MORALITY AND THE BOMB

Morality and the Bomb:

AN ETHICAL ASSESSMENT OF NUCLEAR DETERRENCE

DAVID FISHER

ST. MARTIN'S PRESS
New York

© 1985 David Fisher
All rights reserved. For information, write:
St. Martin's Press, Inc., 175 Fifth Avenue, New York 10010
Printed in Great Britain
First published in the United States of America in 1985

Library of Congress Cataloging in Publication Data
Fisher, David, 1947-
   Morality and the bomb.

   Bibliography: p.
   Includes index.
   1. Deterrence (strategy) — Moral and ethical aspects.
2. Nuclear warfare — Moral and ethical aspects.
I. Title.
U162.6.F5 1985   172'.42   85-2210
ISBN 0-312-54784-6

The views expressed in this book are those of the author alone;
they should not be taken as necessarily reflecting official policy
or thinking.

CONTENTS

To Sophia

ACKNOWLEDGEMENTS

The book was written during the academic year 1983–4 when I had the privilege to be a visiting research fellow at Nuffield College Oxford, on sabbatical leave from the Ministry of Defence. I am grateful to the Ministry of Defence for granting me such leave and to the Warden and Fellows of Nuffield College for their hospitality and support. I have benefited from discussion of the ideas dealt with in the book both in Oxford (where some of them were presented in a series of seminars delivered jointly with Anthony Kenny in Hilary Term 1984) and in London, particularly in the amicable forum provided by the Council on Christian Approaches to Defence and Disarmament. Many friends and colleagues have helped with their comments and criticisms. I should like to record my especial gratitude to Tony Colclough, Les Green, Sir Arthur Hockaday, Michael Howard, Anthony Kenny, Keith Maslin, Barrie Paskins and Frank Roberts. Above all, I wish to record my debt to Michael Quinlan from whose own thinking in this area and from whose help and encouragement I have profited enormously. The errors that remain are my own. The views expressed should not be taken as necessarily reflecting official policy or thinking.

Final thanks go to Jenny Roberts and Elaine Herman who typed and retyped the manuscript with patience and care.

September 1984

1 DETERRENCE

On 6 August 1945 an atomic bomb with the explosive power equivalent to some 13,000 tons of TNT, or 13 kilotons, was dropped by the US Air Force on the city of Hiroshima. At least 66,000 people died almost immediately. Three days later a second bomb of 20 kilotons was dropped on Nagasaki, causing some 40,000 prompt fatalities.

What was the significance of those two atomic detonations in the summer of 1945? Certainly, they marked the arrival of a new and particularly horrifying kind of weapon. But human ingenuity had already devised chemical and biological weapons, with their own distinctive brand of horror. Nor was either attack the most devastating of the Second World War. That dubious distinction belongs to the attack on the south-west portion of Tokyo during the night of 23 May 1945. Within two hours some 520 bombers dropped almost 4,000 tons of incendiary bombs on an area of about eleven square miles, causing deaths estimated to range from 83,000 to over 100,000. Comparable casualty levels had earlier been achieved by the attack on Dresden during the period 13–15 February 1945. What was strikingly different about the attacks on Hiroshima and Nagasaki was that these levels of destruction were achieved in each case almost instantaneously by a single bomb. The summer of 1945 thus heralded the arrival of a weapon of almost boundless destructive power.

The cost of war had been rising since the Napoleonic Wars, as industrialisation made possible the mass production of weapons and the means of transporting and supplying large armies. It had taken a further sharp upwards turn as the arrival of aircraft facilitated the reach of war beyond the battlefield. But with the advent of nuclear weapons, particularly as, in the years following 1945, more and more powerful bombs were produced and, from 1949, by the Soviet Union as well as the West, the inflation line shot off the end of the graph. The cost of all-out war between nuclear powers had become literally unaffordable and not just of nuclear war but conventional as well, given the inherent risk of escalation to the nuclear level from the moment the first conventional shot was fired in any major conflict between nuclear powers.

Nuclear weapons have thus necessitated a radical transformation in thinking about war, as dramatic as the conceptual shifts in the physical sciences from a Ptolemaic geocentric world view to the heliocentric universe of Copernicus or, more recently, from Newtonian physics to the physics of Einstein's relativity theory. Just as in the physical sciences, so in strategy the thought revolution required has entailed a drastic reordering of priorities among concepts, wholesale revision of many of their meanings and the introduction of entirely new concepts. Not surprisingly, the need for this radical conceptual shift has taken time to percolate the military and political establishments and even now does not appear to have taken firm root in some of the outer reaches of the American defence establishment: peripheral areas sometimes, unfortunately, treated by European opponents of nuclear weapons as central. But the need for the Copernican thought revolution was quickly appreciated by some defence specialists and has long been the orthodoxy of NATO thinking. Writing in 1945, shortly after the atomic detonations, the American defence strategist Bernard Brodie declared: 'Thus far the chief purpose of our military establishment has been to win wars. From now its chief purpose must be to avert them.'[1] With the advent of nuclear weapons, the era of deterrence had also dawned.

Deterrence means dissuading an adversary from initiating or continuing military action by posing for him the prospect that the costs of such action would exceed the gains. Deterrence is not a new concept. Military forces have long had some deterrent function. But nuclear weapons have given deterrence an urgent primacy and efficacy never before achieved. This has arisen because of two facts. First, the inflation in the cost of war has produced a manifest and yawning disparity between the costs and gains of aggression. In the pre-nuclear era, the deterrent function of conventional forces was at best uncertain because the prizes of aggression were not self-evidently outweighed by the costs: victory might seem possible and even defeat not intolerable. In the nuclear era this is no longer so. Secondly, and closely related to this, the very concept of a classical military victory has lost its meaning when applied to nuclear warfare. In the pre-nuclear era, the defensive role of conventional forces, once deterrence had failed, was physically to deprive an aggressor of his ability to achieve his objective. In theory, this might be achieved by an impregnable defensive screen but, given the conspicuous lack of success of such Maginot lines, in practice, it has meant depriving the adversary of his physical ability to continue fighting, whether by destroying his military strength or his ability to project that strength. Indeed, this has been the usual criterion for military victory for either an aggressor or defender. It may, of course, not always have been necessary fully to achieve this: the imminent prospect of such deprivation may have sufficed to convince an adversary that the costs of continued fighting outweighed the gains. But the complete physical destruction of the German military machine was required in 1945 to convince Hitler of the necessity of surrender.

The immense power of nuclear weapons and lack of any effective defence against them, together with the development of a multiplicity of highly effective and largely invulnerable delivery systems, particularly those launched from submarines, have rendered obsolete the classical concept of victory. Since at least the early 1960s neither superpower has had any realistic expectation of being able physically to deprive his opponent of the capability to wield military force. It can thus no longer make sense for fighting to continue until the limits of one side's physical capability have been reached. For, however many blows each side could land on the other, vast unspent force would still remain available to each side and the planet would be destroyed long before such power had finally been spent. Mutual annihilation may thus be possible in a conflict between nuclear powers, but a classical military victory is not. In turn, this has meant that manipulation of an adversary's political will, usually characteristic in the pre-nuclear era of the terminal stages of a conflict, must now predominate. The only credible threatened use of nuclear weapons between nuclear powers is not to secure a classical military victory but to operate on the political will of the adversary: to convince him that the costs of military aggression far exceed the gains.

In the early days of the Alliance, deterrence rested primarily on nuclear weapons, reflecting both the initial short-lived Western monopoly and the subsequent more enduring Western reluctance to pay the high cost of seeking to match Soviet conventional force levels. The role assigned to conventional forces under the early policy of 'massive retaliation' was primarily that of providing a trip wire to any Soviet attack, allowing a pause for thought and, hopefully, a negotiated settlement before the power of nuclear weapons was brought to bear. The credibility of a policy that offered so

limited a range of choices ('holocaust or humiliation' as the critical
slogan went) was undermined by the growth of Soviet nuclear
power in the late 1950s and 1960s and, in particular, their
acquisition of their own intercontinental nuclear capability. In 1967
NATO therefore adopted its present strategy of flexible response,
enshrined in the NATO Military Committee document MC 14/3.
'The aim of the Alliance', as the 1983 UK Defence White Paper
stated, 'is to convince the Soviet Union that we have at our disposal
a range of defensive options that would enable us to respond to any
attack at an appropriate level and that any gains which Soviet
aggression might be designed to achieve would be outweighed by
the damage which could be inflicted on them.'[2]

NATO's strategy has always been defensive: as was reaffirmed in
the June 1982 Bonn Summit declaration, none of the Alliance's
weapons — conventional or nuclear — would ever be used except in
response to attack. The aim is, moreover, to prevent not just
nuclear but any war, given the immense destructiveness of even
conventional warfare, as evidenced by the major conflicts of this
century, and the inherent risk, already noted, of nuclear escalation
from the onset of a conventional conflict in Europe. Should the
fundamental aim of preventing war fail, the objective would be to
stop the conflict as quickly as possible at the lowest level, by con-
vincing the aggressor that he had miscalculated the balance of
advantage and that by continuing the conflict he would be running
unacceptable risks. Thus, even were fighting to occur, deterrence
would remain the goal.

In order to implement the strategy, the Alliance needs forces,
equipment and plans for their use to provide the necessary range of
options for dealing with aggression. In the first instance, the key
requirement is for sufficient conventional forces to deter an attack
at the conventional level by providing a manifest ability to conduct
a robust conventional defence. But since a conventional defence,
even if successful, could always be overcome by an adversary's use
or threatened use of nuclear weapons, a capability to offer a
credible response to a variety of nuclear threats — whether at the
theatre or strategic level — is also needed. This generates the
requirement for both theatre and strategic nuclear weapons and
targeting plans for their use to provide a wide measure of choice,
extending from the most limited theatre nuclear release up to the
strategic level.

Indeed, even at the strategic level, credible deterrence requires a range of options for use. It is sometimes assumed that the only US policy for strategic use would be massive, reflexive attacks on Soviet cities and nuclear forces. This misapprehension was initially prompted by Foster Dulles's 'instant massive retaliation' speech of May 1952 but was subsequently kept alive, even after the official demise of the policy of massive retaliation, by Robert McNamara's public definition of deterrence in 1964 in terms of the ability to inflict mutual assured destruction (instantly eliciting the critical acronym MAD): a level of destruction variously defined by McNamara as between 20 and 33 per cent of the Soviet population and 50 and 75 per cent of industrial capacity.

In fact, however, apart from the earliest days of the nuclear era when poor intelligence, scarcity of bombs and lack of any means for their accurate delivery meant there was little choice but to target cities, US operational plans have always included a variety of target options, progressively refined and developed as better intelligence, more weapons and more accurate delivery systems became available. The current US Single Integrated Operational Plan is estimated by Desmond Ball to contain some 40,000 potential target installations, embracing a wide variety of target types: conventional military forces, stockpiles, bases and installations; nuclear forces; political and administrative centres; and economic and industrial centres.[3] Moreover, since at least 1974 successive US administrations have consistently made clear in their public pronouncements the importance they attach to having a range of options for selective strategic use alternative to an all-out counter-offensive against cities, with priority given to military targets. In his 1974 report to Congress as Secretary of Defense under President Nixon, James Schlesinger stressed the need for 'a series of measured responses to aggression which have some relation to the provocation, have prospects of terminating hostilities before general nuclear war breaks out and leaves some possibility for restoring deterrence'.[4] Selectivity was also stressed in President Carter's Presidential Directive 59 of July 1980, while William Clark, then national security adviser to President Reagan, explained in 1983 that current targeting policy is to 'hold at risk the war-making capability of the Soviet Union — its armed forces, and the industrial capacity to sustain war'.[5] The British Government has stated that its 'concept of deterrence is concerned essentially with posing a potential threat to key aspects of Soviet state power'.[6]

I have thus far sought to explain the rationale and development of NATO's policy of deterrence. But what, if any, is the basis for believing that deterrence is effective in helping to prevent war and, even if it has been so far, that it will continue to work? To answer these questions, it is necessary to explore further the underlying logic of deterrence.

In the light of the earlier discussion, it is possible to specify the conditions under which mutual deterrence holds firm as follows:

Nuclear powers A and B are mutually deterred from attacking each other if and only if:

(i) Each side has the ability, if attacked by the other, to inflict on the attacker sufficient harm to outweigh any conceivable gain to be secured from the attack.

(ii) Neither side can rule out that the other might use this ability, if attacked.

Provided both conditions are fully met, neither power can rationally attack the other.

Let us now consider in what circumstances these conditions would be fully satisfied.

Under the first scenario, both A and B possess an invulnerable intercontinental strategic nuclear retaliatory capability but no other military forces.[7] Given that any use of such weapons would be horrific and carry a risk of escalation to an even more horrendous level, condition (i) would clearly be met. It is also reasonable to suppose that condition (ii) is met, particularly since, as formulated, this merely requires that neither side can rule out that the other might use nuclear weapons, if attacked — not that either has to believe this will happen: a formulation justified by what Michael Howard has dubbed Healey's Theorem, 'if there is one chance in a hundred of nuclear weapons being used, the odds would be enough to deter an aggressor even if they were not enough to reassure an ally'.[8] Both conditions are thus met and an equilibrium of force is established under which it would be irrational for either side to initiate military action against the other.

Secondly, let us suppose that B, and only B, acquires a conventional capability. As before, stalemate persists at the strategic level but B might now calculate that A would not risk a strategic response to a conventional attack: he might, that is, come to doubt the validity of condition (ii). Some instability has thus been introduced and B might deem it rational to initiate military action, at the conventional level, against A.

In order to restore stability, let us, thirdly, suppose that A also acquires conventional weapons. The strategic stalemate still persists. Furthermore, neither A nor B can now afford a conventional attack on the other both because of the resistance that could be offered at that level and because of the risk that any major conventional conflict could escalate to the nuclear level.

Fourthly, some instability might be reintroduced if B, and only B, were to acquire theatre nuclear weapons. As before, the strategic stalemate persists but B might just calculate that he could now use his assumed military superiority at the sub-strategic level to secure a quick victory over A (using his theatre nuclear monopoly to overcome any successful conventional resistance), judging that A would not risk strategic retaliation. This would be an immensely hazardous judgement for B to make, particularly given the weak formulation of condition (ii). But to remove any prospect that B might thus reason, A could well deem it prudent to acquire his own theatre nuclear capability.

We have thus reached the fifth and final scenario under which both A and B possess the full spectrum of strategic, theatre nuclear and conventional forces. As in all previous options, the strategic stalemate persists. It would also be irrational for either A or B to attack the other with conventional forces both because of the resistance they would encounter at that level and the risk that a conventional conflict could escalate to the theatre nuclear and, hence, to the strategic level. Nuclear weapons thus do not merely deter use of other nuclear weapons, they also massively enhance the deterrent effect which conventional weapons themselves possess.

Under this scenario, stability is thus finally and fully restored. Both conditions (i) and (ii) are met and it would be irrational for either A or B to initiate military action against the other. So long as the conditions remain fulfilled, nuclear weapons are thus rationally unusable by either side against the other.

This scenario does, of course, correspond to the current balance of power between NATO and the Warsaw Pact. The equilibrium of force that has been established between these alliances and their respective nuclear superpowers means that it would be irrational for either power bloc to initiate military action against the other's vital interests. In Europe these vital interests have, moreover, been carefully delimited and defined, particularly by the important 1975 Helsinki Agreement, which formally ruled out any change, other than by peaceful and mutual agreement, to the existing territorial division of the continent. Military force may still be usable by a superpower elsewhere in the world where the other nuclear superpower's interests may not be engaged (e.g. Vietnam, Afghanistan). But even here, each side has been and is likely to remain deterred from using nuclear weapons even against a non-nuclear power not only because of the global political repercussions of use against a non-nuclear state but also because of the possible reaction of the other nuclear superpower. Nuclear weapons thus contribute powerfully to the prevention of war. From the West's viewpoint they thus both help to secure the illimitable blessing of peace and, at the same time, ensure that the West does not fall under the political domination of an alien totalitarian power, whether as a result of direct attack or the more subtle coercion which a nuclear power could exert over a non-nuclear power to secure political or military advantage by the process which has been termed 'nuclear blackmail'.

The stability of deterrence depends on a balance of military power but this concept, as with so many others, has undergone a significant change of meaning in the nuclear era. Traditionally, a conventional balance of power required that each side's forces should be broadly matched in both quantity and quality. For only thus could each side be confident of his capability physically to deny the other the ability to achieve the objectives of his aggression. But neither of these requirements needs to be satisfied to achieve nuclear equilibrium. At the nuclear level, the only balance required is that each side should retain the assured and credible ability to inflict unacceptable damage on the other. This ability is not necessarily impaired by one side's superiority in both the quantity and quality of its nuclear forces, as evidenced by the serious regard held for the Soviet Union's retaliatory capability in the 1950s and early 1960s, even though Western nuclear forces were then superior in both respects to those of the Soviet Union. Very wide fluctuations, particularly in numbers, can be tolerated without the nuclear balance being upset. The balance of power in the nuclear era is inherently more stable and less prone to disturbance by arms racing to achieve quantitative superiority than is a conventional balance.

None the less, mutual deterrence could cease to work if either of the conditions for mutual deterrence were no longer satisfied. I shall consider three major ways in which the equilibrium that has been established might be disturbed.

First, condition (i), which requires that each side should have the ability to inflict on the other damage sufficient to outweigh the gains of aggression, would become invalid if one side ceased to have this ability. This could come about if one of the nuclear powers unilaterally disarmed or allowed the effectiveness of its nuclear capability to decay. If that happened, it could well appear rational for the remaining nuclear power to use or threaten to use its nuclear monopoly against the non-nuclear power. Indeed, the only time nuclear weapons have ever been used — some 40 years ago — was by a nuclear power against a non-nuclear power.

Secondly, mutual deterrence could cease to work if one side came to believe that the other side, even though still in possession of the weapons, would never use them: in that case condition (ii), which requires that neither side can rule out that the other might use his nuclear capability, would become invalid. This might occur in various ways. One way might be if the Soviet Union came to believe the sincere declarations of non-use which, for reasons we shall examine in Chapter 6, have been urged on NATO by various commentators. Another would be if the Soviet Union came to doubt that the United States was still offering Europe the protection of its strategic nuclear umbrella. This might perhaps arise because of a decay in the political cohesion of the Alliance and a rift between Europe and the USA or because the Soviets had succeeded in achieving a monopoly of theatre nuclear weapons whose use, confined to the European landmass, they judged would not provoke US strategic retaliation, since this would put at risk the US homeland.

If — for whatever reason — the Soviet Union had thus come to doubt that the West would use its nuclear weapons, they might be tempted to launch an attack on Europe, judging that the gains would outweigh the costs. And if that happened, Alliance policy envisages that it might then be rational for NATO, in the face of imminent defeat, to authorise a limited use of nuclear weapons in order to re-establish deterrence, by demonstrating to the Soviet Union that they had miscalculated the probable balance of profit and loss. Moreover, once an attack has occurred, an asymmetry then develops between the profit and loss calculus of each side. So long as the conditions for stable mutual deterrence remain satisfied, each side is deterred from attacking the other by the knowledge that the costs of such action would outweigh the gains.

But once aggression has occurred, what is at stake for the attacker is still the balance between the costs and gains of an attack; for the defender, however, about to be over-borne by aggression, what matters is what is to be gained by continued defence and what is to be lost by surrender. In such circumstances, the defender may be expected to place a higher valuation on the protection of his home-land and way of life than does the aggressor on the prize to be secured by his aggression.

The third way in which mutual deterrence could be eroded would be if one side achieved an ability physically to enforce the invalidity of condition (i), whether by physically disarming the other's nuclear capability by a 'first strike' or by neutralising the capability by means of a defensive screen against missile attack, as envisaged by President Reagan's concept of 'strategic defence'.[9] If either possibility were realisable, the side possessing such a capability might deem the use of nuclear weapons rational. Moreover, the side threatened by a disarming first strike might be tempted to prevent it by getting in first and destroying as much as it could of the other's nuclear capability.

These then are the three main ways in which mutual deterrence between the superpowers might cease to hold. Is there any risk of any of them being fulfilled? The answer is surely not. Neither side has disarmed or intends to disarm unilaterally, thereby rendering condition (i) invalid. On the contrary, both are maintaining the effectiveness of their nuclear capabilities. As regards condition (ii), the political cohesion and stability of NATO remain strong and the Soviet Union can have no reasonable ground for doubting the con-tinued validity of the US nuclear umbrella or the continued linkage of US strategic forces to the defence of Europe, guaranteed by both the presence in Europe of numerous US troops and the deployment in Europe of theatre nuclear weapons. (Indeed, even if they did, they would still have to reckon on the independent nuclear forces of both France and the United Kingdom.) Moreover, for such doubts to have any effect on the stability of the deterrent they would need to be very strong indeed to invalidate condition (ii). For, as I have carefully specified that condition, it merely requires that neither side can rule out that the other might use its nuclear capability, if attacked.

The third way in which deterrence might fail would be by one side acquiring the capability to enforce the invalidity of condition (i), either by neutralising the other side's nuclear capability by a defensive screen or by the physical destruction of its capability. Strategic defence is, at present, only a long-term research objective and the deployment of such defensive systems is constrained by the 1972 Anti-Ballistic Missile (ABM) Treaty. The concept is not realisable within the foreseeable future and, indeed, attainment of such a goal by either side is likely to prove as elusive and the pursuit, if continued, as wasteful as the search in the 1950s and 1960s for the perfect ABM system. For the destructiveness of nuclear weapons is such that if only a few missiles could penetrate the screen — a possibility neither side could confidently rule out, given the technical ingenuity and effort that would no doubt be applied to countering the defensive network and the impracticality of an effective comprehensive test of the system — immense damage would still be wreaked. Moreover, even if — *per impossibile* — the system could provide a 100 per cent permanent guarantee against ballistic missile attack, each nuclear superpower would still remain vulnerable to highly destructive nuclear attacks delivered by other means. There thus appears no realistic prospect of strategic defence enforcing the invalidity of condition (i).

The fear that undoubtedly fuels much of the peace movement's protests is that one side might acquire a first-strike capability, that is, the ability physically to destroy the other's nuclear capability by a pre-emptive attack.

Two developments are usually cited in support of such fear: first, the greater precision and accuracy with which missiles can now be aimed and secondly, the public avowal, noted earlier, by successive recent US administrations of targeting options which avoid direct attacks on population centres. Prima facie, these developments should be applauded since it can only be a moral gain to move away from large bombs inaccurately aimed at cities. In the early nuclear era large weapons were designed to compensate for the then inaccuracy of aiming techniques. The increased precision made possible by current technology has permitted a massive reduction in the explosive power of the US stockpile: the megatonnage of all US nuclear weapons is now only 25 per cent of what it was in 1960.

None the less, the fear remains that such developments have brought nearer the prospect of a first-strike capability. But to suppose this is totally to fail to understand the nature of nuclear weapons. The combination of the immense power of nuclear weapons, together with the multiplicity and elusiveness of the delivery systems and lack of any effective defence against them, has, as argued earlier, quite drained of meaning the concept of military victory achieved by nuclear attack. And this has come about precisely because neither side can have any realistic expectation of physically depriving the other of his ability to wield such force. The concept of a first strike aimed at achieving this impossible goal is thus quite incoherent, while to secure any lesser objective would be irrational. Thus, for example, even if — as many would doubt — the increased accuracy of the current generation of Soviet missiles enabled them totally to destroy all the land-based US intercontinental ballistic missiles (ICBMs), there would seem no possible point in so doing, when the US air-launched and, in particular, submarine-launched systems would remain intact. The fact is that neither side is, or within the foreseeable future is likely to be, in a position to deliver a knock-out blow against the other's nuclear capability. It is for this reason that the first strike option remains a chimera.

The effectiveness and stability of the central deterrent thus remains assured. But doubts may persist on two grounds. First, the model of deterrence I have presented presupposes the rationality of the actors. Is this a safe assumption and, even if it is, might nuclear war still not occur by accident, rather than rational design? Secondly, the model, as described, is between two players or teams of players. Might it not be invalidated by nuclear proliferation? Let us address each of these in turn.

The degree of rationality presupposed by the model is of a fairly elementary kind. Deterrence theorists may sometimes embellish their texts with an elaborate filigree of complex argumentation but this is often needlessly obscurantist. No great intellectual subtlety is required to grasp the central and brutal equation of deterrence, that the cost of aggression between nuclear powers would far exceed the gains.

As regards the safety of the central deterrent from upset by accident or the intrusion of a rogue lunatic, very considerable efforts have been made over the last half century, and continue to be made, to eliminate such risks as far as is possible. The NATO procedures for nuclear release are complex and cumbersome, in no instance entrusted to one individual; they require an elaborate system of checks and cross-checks, and, in the case of most theatre-based systems, physical impediments to release by electronic locking devices ('Permissive Action Links'), until the appropriate political authorisation is received. Hotlines are regularly exercised and updated. There are a host of practical agreements between the superpowers to enhance the safety of the system, including, for example, advance notification of missile launch tests whose purpose might otherwise be misunderstood. Intelligence, especially by satellite photography, has greatly increased each side's knowledge of what the other is about.

Moreover, all these practical safeguards continue fully to operate even when, as in the past few years, general political relations between the superpowers have been strained. It is highly desirable that political relations should be improved and the full range of arms control negotiations vigorously resumed. But it remains none the less true that, despite the regrettable cooling of *détente* and the sometimes ill-advised rhetoric, the superpowers have continued in their actual behaviour to exercise massive restraint and caution. When the Soviet Union invaded Afghanistan or imposed the crushing of Solidarity in Poland, the West did not intervene, any more than did the Soviet Union when the USA invaded Grenada. Each side has thus continued to respect the other's sphere of influence, while the boundaries of these have, with the passage of time, become more clearly defined, particularly, as already noted, in the case of Europe by the 1975 Helsinki Agreement.

Of more valid concern is, therefore, undoubtedly the risk of nuclear proliferation. The nuclear superpowers are mutually deterred because each knows that the other possesses an invulnerable retaliatory capability which might be used in the event of attack. But these conditions for stable mutual deterrence may not be fulfilled by new arrivals to the nuclear club who may lack the technical competence to assure the invulnerability of their weapons and may be less well schooled than the established members in the restraint and caution which membership requires, particularly if in dispute with non-nuclear regional rivals. Nuclear proliferation has, however, not occurred to anything like the extent expected by many forecasters: the last applicant for membership of the nuclear club was China in 1964 and her capability remains limited. India's 'peaceful' nuclear explosion of 1974 has so far not led to her acquisition of either a bomb or delivery system. These facts reflect not only the beneficial effects of the 1968 Non-Proliferation Treaty but also the very mixed blessings of a nuclear capability. For any country contemplating entry to the nuclear club would not only face immense international pressures against so doing but would also have to reckon, quite apart from the financial cost, on the

very severe limitation of its freedom of action which membership
— willy nilly — imposes: the penalties of mistakes in the nuclear
era are prohibitively high, particularly as the behaviour of any new
member would inevitably attract the very close scrutiny of the
nuclear superpowers.

The worry none the less persists that others may yet seek to
acquire a nuclear capability, may, indeed, as is widely conjectured
to be the case with Israel, already secretly be well on the way to this.
This fear obviously lends urgency to the need to strengthen the
safeguards governing transmission to third parties of nuclear
technology and materials usable for military purposes. It also
underlines the need for greater efforts by the superpowers to fulfil
their obligations under the Non-Proliferation Treaty to reduce their
nuclear stockpiles.

All this and more can be conceded, but the question still remains
whether the risk of nuclear proliferation casts doubt on the validity
of the central deterrent. The answer is surely that it does not. The
concern that nuclear weapons might spread without being accompanied by stable mutual deterrence is not an argument against
deterrence. The existing nuclear powers have responsibilities to
reduce the risk of such proliferation, but that risk derives from the
availability of nuclear knowledge and materials rather than from
the existence of the central deterrent. The arrival of nuclear third
parties, which it is to be hoped, in any case, can be thus minimised,
would not in any way invalidate the conditions that underpin the
mutual deterrence that holds between the superpowers. It would,
thus, not derogate from the beneficial effects of the central deterrent in preventing war between the two major power blocs that
bestride the world. Moreover, any nuclear third party would not
only be deterred — by the operation of those same conditions —
from trying nuclear conclusions with an existing nuclear power,
they would also need to consider very carefully before contemplating the use of nuclear weapons against a non-nuclear regional
rival what would be the reaction of the nuclear superpowers to such
a flagrant breach of the well-entrenched 'tradition for their non-
use'.[10] Finally, the central deterrent, by imposing caution on the
behaviour of the superpowers not only towards each other but — as
noted earlier — elsewhere in the globe, helps to act as a restraint on
proliferation. In the absence of stable mutual deterrence between
the superpowers, a superpower left wielding nuclear force unconstrained by the other superpower might be able to exploit his

nuclear monopoly not only against the other superpower and his allies but third parties as well, the case for whose acquisition of their own nuclear weapons might be correspondingly increased. The ability of most countries to have effective non-nuclear defence policies in a world in which nuclear weapons exist is to that extent parasitic upon the very success of the central deterrent in neutralising the usability of that nuclear force.

I therefore conclude that the central deterrent is both effective and stable. If it is not entirely risk-free, the recognition of this fact does itself help impose further restraint: as Bernard Brodie has remarked, 'Under these circumstances one does not tempt fate.'[11]

NATO's policy of deterrence thus appears to provide a robust and reliable means of helping to prevent war, while preserving our political independence. We must turn now to the central question with which this book is concerned: can it possibly be moral, given the savage destructiveness of the weapons upon whose threatened use it ultimately relies?

Many critics have argued that it can not because it breaches moral principles enshrined in the just war tradition. I shall therefore begin the assessment of the morality of nuclear deterrence by examining the validity and scope of the just war tradition.

2 THE JUST WAR TRADITION I

I shall start my evaluation of the just war tradition by briefly stating what it says and then considering whether such an antique theory can have any possible relevance to politics in the latter half of the twentieth century. The theory is not marked out by a single and definitive list of rules and prescriptions. Rather, it is embodied in a living tradition, developed from a variety of sources and still under development. Depending on the author consulted, different features of the theory may be given prominence, but there is a general consensus that the theory includes the following elements.

The theory presupposes that there is a prima facia moral presumption against war: war stands in need of justification. War is a moral tragedy: an 'accursed thyng and not due' in Christine de Pisan's phrase.[1] It is therefore morally permissible if and only if certain conditions are met. These conditions relate first to the circumstances in which a state may legitimately have to resort to war — the *jus ad bellum*; and secondly, to the way in which the war should be conducted — the *jus in bello*.

The *jus ad bellum* prescribes that war is permissible if and only if:

(a) war is declared by a competent authority;
(b) as a last resort, all available peaceful means of settling the dispute having first been tried and failed;
(c) for the sake of a just cause;
(d) the harm judged likely to result from the war is not disproportionate to the likely good to be achieved, taking into account the probability of success.

The *jus in bello* adds two further conditions governing the conduct of war:

(e) the harm judged likely to result from a particular military action should not be disproportionate to the good aimed at;
(f) non-combatants should be immune from direct attack.

16

The two sets of conditions are, to an extent, logically independent: one may conduct a just war unjustly or an unjust war justly. But for a war to be just *tout court*, all six conditions need to be met. Quite how strictly they all need to be met is a matter of dispute within the tradition. This dilemma arises because war is an activity extended over often considerable periods of time and engaging large numbers of participants. Thus, even if all six conditions are, in general, satisfied, occasional lapses by some participants may occur. If so, would they invalidate the overall justice of the war? My view is that this would be an unreasonably strict requirement and that, depending on their precise nature, occasional lapses need not necessarily preclude the overall justice of the war. But such lapses and their authors would still be subject to individual moral condemnation.

This, in bald outline, is what the theory states. Its origins are usually traced at least as far back as St Augustine and, often, further into classical antiquity. St Augustine wrestled in the fifth century A.D. with the perennial question whether a Christian may engage in war without sin, seeking to reconcile the pacific teaching of Christ in the Sermon on the Mount with the apparently divinely approved bellicosity of the Jewish nation in the Old Testament. The theory was then further developed in the middle ages by canon lawyers such as Gratian (twelfth century) and theologians such as Aquinas (thirteenth century). It was brought to fruition in the sixteenth and seventeenth centuries by writers such as Vitoria, Suarez and Grotius.[2] It was then largely neglected, except in Catholic seminaries, until its revival in the latter half of this century, particularly as a result of the work of the American theologians Father John Ford and Paul Ramsey.[3] It now provides the underlying premises for most philosophical and theological discussion of the morality of war, as witnessed by the recent Pastoral Letter on War and Peace of the US Catholic Bishops[4] and the Anglican Working Party Report, *The Church and the Bomb*.[5]

In view of the antecedents of the theory in medieval Christian and chivalric traditions, it may be tempting to dismiss its relevance to a world from which chivalry has long since departed and in which the post-Christian Western democracies are aligned against an anti-Christian Marxist dictatorship. This would be mistaken. For, although the theory was primarily (but by no means exclusively) motivated by Christian concerns, it was developed within the natural law tradition of the church. Its prescriptions are not based on divine fiats but rather justified by reason and are presented to be of appeal to men of reason anywhere. They need, therefore, to be judged on their own merits.

Nor should the relevance of the theory be summarily dismissed as yet another conceptual casualty of the Copernican thought revolution, described in the last chapter, which the advent of nuclear weapons has required. I shall be examining in Chapter 6 a particular version of this argument that seeks to separate the moral evaluation of deterrence from that of nuclear warfare. But it would appear fallacious summarily to reject the theory by any general argument that modern war, even at the conventional level, can inherently know no bounds: that war is an evil to be avoided but, if it occurs, it is, in General Sherman's phrase, 'hell' which only the naive and unrealistic would suppose could be subject to moral restraint. This is the 'war is hell' brand of ethical nihilism, ably criticised by Michael Walzer in his book *Just and Unjust Wars*.[6] It rests on the mistake of treating war as if it were a natural force — like a forest fire — beyond good and evil. On the contrary, war is an activity started and carried on by human beings and, like any other human activity, is subject to moral criticism and restraint. The key question is whether the just war tradition has adequately described the relevant moral rules.

The third general objection to the modern relevance of the just war theory is that its basic presumption against war is unrealistic, given the frequency and, indeed, the inevitability of war within post-lapsarian human society. But the theory is not based on a naive assumption of the instant perfectibility of mankind. Rather, it recognises only too clearly the likelihood and, indeed, occasional necessity of conflict, given man's all too apparent fallibility and the consequent need for force sometimes to be used to constrain the ambitions of wicked men, lest the innocent should suffer. It is this recognition that war is always possible, and may sometimes be necessary, which lends urgency to the theory's demand for restraint in war.

The moral presumption against war rests simply on the fact that war causes immense human suffering, the extent of which may be difficult to control once a war has started. And this fact is surely difficult to gainsay. Indeed, one of the principal reasons for the recent revival of the just war tradition is precisely because our experience, even of conventional war in this century, has vividly and horrendously underlined this perennial truth, to which the advent of nuclear weapons has added even sharper focus. It is for this reason that the just war theory insists that war should only be started for very good reason and should then be conducted with restraint. But the insistence that war stands in need of justification does not mean that war can never be morally justified. On the contrary, it is a key feature of the theory that war, on occasion, may not merely be morally permissible: it may be a moral duty. The point was well stressed by St Augustine at the start of the tradition: 'it is the wrongdoing of the opposing party which compels the wise man to wage just war'.[7] One of the aims of the just war tradition is to specify when this may be so.

It is not, therefore, profitable summarily to dismiss the just war theory as outmoded. We need to evaluate the theory in terms of its specific content and to this task I now turn.

My evaluation will be undertaken against a presumption that morality is not an irrational activity bound by a set of inscrutable absolute prescriptions. On the contrary, moral rules can and should be justified by reference to their contribution to the promotion of human welfare and the reduction of suffering, neither of which can be sensibly encompassed within the narrow confines of utilitarian hedonism. Those fond of labels will call this a consequentialist viewpoint, and so they may, in so far as I regard consequences as crucial to any ethical evaluation. Mankind has never been able to afford the luxury of exalting personal moral integrity to the neglect of consequences: *fiat justitia, ruat caelum* ('let justice be done, though the heavens fall'), as the Latin proverb goes. Still less can we do so in the nuclear era, when the all too literal collapse of the heavens is among the consequences that must be avoided. But, although consequences are thus crucial, I am not thereby committed to depreciating the value of fundamental moral principles that encapsulate the accumulated moral wisdom of mankind nor yet to the outsider's view of ethics characteristic of extreme utilitarianism: the view that all there is to moral judgement is the detached, impartial, scientific calculation of the consequences of action, unconstrained by the beliefs, desires and intentions of the participants. On the contrary, these too play an important role in moral judgement. Any balanced ethical judgement thus needs to address both the internal and external aspects of action: the mental states of the agent and the consequences of his agency.

Let us now examine in turn each of the requirements of the just war theory.

The first requirement, that war be declared by a competent authority, is justified by Aquinas as follows:

> A private individual may not declare war; for he can have recourse to the judgment of a superior to safeguard his rights. Nor has he the right to mobilize the people, which is necessary in war. But since responsibility for public affairs is entrusted to the rulers, it is they who are charged with the defence of the city, realm or province subject to them. And just as in the punishment of criminals they rightly defend the state against all internal disturbance with the civil arm . . . So also they have the duty of defending the state, with the weapons of war, against external enemies.[8]

Aquinas was writing in a feudal and hierarchical society long since departed. But the key features of his argument, suitably rephrased to suit modern conditions, would still appear reasonable. A government has not merely a right but a duty to provide for the internal and external security of the realm. That right cannot be entrusted to individuals, for war vitally affects the interests of a people as a whole whether for good or ill: only a government lawfully constituted to represent those interests should be entitled to declare war. Moreover, only a government has the ability to mobilise the resources necessary to wage modern war. As thus expressed, the argument for competent authority seems unobjectionable, although it would need to be supplemented by a theory of just rebellion to allow for cases in which a government is so oppressive and unjust that there may be a good reason for a people to seek its overthrow, if necessary by violent means. The development of such a theory is beyond the purview of this work.

This condition is sometimes supplemented in the medieval tradition by the requirement that there should be a formal declaration of war. In general, more recent exponents of the theory have dropped this condition (*The Church and the Bomb* being an interesting exception), partly in recognition that formal declarations of war are now more honoured in the breach than the observance. In any case, it can be argued that this is 'a requirement of decency rather than of justice — to make war without giving notice is unsporting; but it does not follow that the war itself is unjust'.[9]

The next requirement, that war should only be undertaken as a last resort, again seems eminently reasonable. Given the appalling suffering that wars, particularly modern wars, can cause, it is clearly justifiable to insist that governments should not embark upon them lightly but only if all other available methods of resolving the dispute have first been genuinely tried and have failed.

The third condition is that there should be a just cause for the war; that the war should be undertaken for the sake of this cause and, once it has been satisfied, the aim should be to restore peace: these latter qualifications are usually cited as evidence of the 'right intention'. Vitoria defines a just cause as follows: 'there is one and only one just cause for waging war viz. an injury received'.[10]

In medieval theory the just cause was the critical requirement to be met. In much modern writing this condition has been considerably depreciated, if not neglected altogether. The recent and, as I shall argue, mistaken decline of the importance of this condition reflects, in part, difficulties with the concept of just cause perceived even in the heyday of the theory: in particular, the problem grappled with by authors such as Vitoria, Suarez and Grotius that both combatants might seem to have right on their side, the problem, that is, of 'simultaneous ostensible justice'.[11]

In medieval Christendom, when most of Europe shared a common cultural and ethical tradition, it was easier to suppose that only one side in a just war would be clearly perceived — at least by the 'good and wise'[12] — to have a just cause. Even then, this supposition had its inherent difficulties. These difficulties have been sharply exacerbated with the break-up of Christendom and the birth of the modern culturally and ethically pluralist society. According to the just war theory, only one side can have a just cause, if the war is just: a dispute in which both participants had equally legitimate grounds for grievance would not be a just war. But even though at most only one side can have a just cause, it is all too easy for each side in a modern dispute to claim justice on its side and all too difficult, in the absence of effective international machinery for settling such disputes, to decide who, if anyone, is in the right.

For this reason, some authors deny the concept any longer has substantive content and reduce it to a largely procedural requirement, 'that each side should make plain precisely what he takes a just cause to consist in, and why he takes that to constitute a just cause'.[13] The US Catholic bishops, while still perhaps allowing some substance to the concept, have qualified it by the further

condition they have added to the usual just war criteria which they
have called 'comparative justice'. They explain:

The category of comparative justice is designed to emphasize the
presumption against war which stands at the beginning of just
war teaching. In a world of sovereign states recognizing neither a
common moral authority nor a central political authority, comparative justice stresses that no state should act on the basis that
it has 'absolute justice' on its side. Every party to a conflict
should acknowledge the limits of its 'just cause' and the consequent requirement to use *only* limited means in pursuit of its
objectives.[14]

The caution advised by the US Catholic bishops is no doubt
salutary. But recognition of the very real problem posed by
'simultaneous ostensible justice' surely does not warrant a slide
into an ethical relativism in which no clear distinction between rival
values can ever be discerned. Numerous alleged just causes have no
doubt been unjust but some causes have been just and sometimes it
has been possible clearly to perceive this to be so. Many, including
the present author, would regard the protection of humanity
against the monstrous tyranny of Nazism in the last world war as a
paradigmatic just cause, the justice of which no consideration of
ethical or cultural pluralism should be allowed to obscure. Moreover, the defence of Western democratic societies from external
aggression, should this ever occur, by a totalitarian Marxist regime,
deeply hostile to political and religious freedom, would, prima
facie, constitute a just cause by the canons of the just war tradition.
    A further, and closely related, objection to the concept of just
cause is that it leaves it open to the would-be belligerent to place
such value on the justice of his cause as to license any moral
enormity in its defence. But this objection not only overlooks the
other conditions prescribed by the just war tradition, including
those addressed to the conduct of the war; it also fails to appreciate
the restrictive nature of the concept of just cause. In Vitoria's
phrase, 'there is only one just cause for waging war viz. an injury
received'. And, at least in modern international law, this is
interpreted very narrowly to refer to a specific act of external
aggression against the territory of a sovereign state: an act which
both threatens the rights of those whose territory is invaded and *eo
ipso* also weakens the general stability of international society.

Thus interpreted, the concept of just cause clearly rules out any war of territorial conquest or any war undertaken for religious or secular crusades: for example, to 'roll back' Communism or to export freedom and democracy. The only legitimate aim recognised by the just war theory is to rectify the injury received and to restore a stable peace: in Walzer's memorable dictum, 'resistance, restoration and reasonable prevention'.[15] A war, started for a just cause, whose objectives subsequently expand to include unjust ends (for example, territorial aggrandisement) thereby ceases to be just: the war has to be fought for the sake of the just cause. Of course, if the aggression against which one is defending oneself is of a particularly horrendous and determined kind, such as the Nazi threat that so nearly engulfed the world little more than 40 years ago, the amount of resistance that may be required to overcome it can be very great. But that reflects not a weakness of just war theory so much as of mankind that can fashion and support so monstrous an ideology.

Indeed, a more reasonable criticism of the concept of just cause is that, as thus interpreted, it is too restrictive, since it would rule out any pre-emptive attack to prevent external invasion, even when the evidence of imminent aggression was clear and overwhelming (as some would claim was the case prior to the Israeli attack in 1967 that initiated the Six Day War). It would also preclude humanitarian intervention even when genocide was being committed (for example by the Pol Pot regime in Cambodia). To allow for such cases some relaxation of the requirement may perhaps be justified, provided it is kept as minimal as possible: for it is precisely the restrictive nature of the concept of just cause that makes it attractive in an era when war can be so immensely destructive. Moreover, the converse of this argument must certainly be conceded: a state, even if attacked, does not *eo ipso* have a just cause, if its threatening and provocative or genocidal behaviour invited such attack.

The next condition of the just war theory — the principle of proportion — makes clear that, even if the cause is just, this does not license a war in which the probable harm is judged likely to exceed the good achieved, taking into account the probability of success. This condition seems reasonable. Even if one's cause is just, war causes human suffering and, if the suffering is likely to exceed the good aimed at, the war should not be undertaken: as Vitoria notes, 'one must beware lest greater evils follow from the war itself than are avoided by the war'.[16]

The probability of success is normally treated as a separate condition in the literature. I have treated it as an adjunct to the principle of proportion because any assessment of the overall balance between benefits and disbenefits likely to accrue from a war must inevitably be weighted by the probabilities of the various outcomes and, hence, take into account the probability of success. Moreover, treating the probability requirement as part of the principle of proportion also helps elucidate the problem with which some commentators have wrestled as to how much probability of success is required before war can justly be declared. For this, in my formulation, clearly depends on the values assigned to the various outcomes. Thus, if the benefits to be secured by successful resistance to aggression are very high, it may be rational to resist — despite the costs of resistance and the relatively low chance of success — since the aggregate net expected value may still be preferable to the very certain and great disbenefits entailed by non-resistance. But if the chances of success are known to be zero, such a hopeless resistance would not thereby be justified. This was the kind of appalling calculation that faced some of the smaller countries in the last world war in deciding whether or not to try to resist Nazi aggression. Even so, heroic and nigh hopeless resistance is not thereby precluded altogether since, even if the loss of one's own territory is deemed inevitable, one may still reasonably judge it as some kind of success to delay the enemy's advance for a while, in order to buy time for one's neighbours and allies to prepare their defences.

Two main objections can be made against the principle of proportion. First, it may be objected that it lacks sufficient substance since it leaves it open to the would-be belligerents to specify what goods and evils are to be weighed in the balance and what values to attach to them. But this criticism must either assume that the concept of just cause itself lacks substance, a position I have already rejected, or else it must simply mistakenly ignore the role which the concept of the just cause plays in defining what can legitimately be regarded as a good to be aimed at by the war. The evils of war — the human suffering it causes — which are to be placed on the other side of the balance sheet need, of course, no elaboration.

A more serious criticism is that the kind of god-like calculation required to draw up such a balance sheet before the onset of war is beyond the wit of man, given the uncertainty and unpredictability of war and the incommensurability of the values to be thus balanced. What probabilities are to be assigned to the possible outcomes? How many lives is it worth sacrificing successfully to defend a people's right to live in the land and society of their own choosing? Such questions are daunting, indeed, and must inevitably give pause to any sane person contemplating resort to war. But despite all the upsets of war, the conditions under which the decision has to be made are not those of complete uncertainty: a nation faced with armed aggression knows what values are at stake and has some idea, at least, of what risks are likely to be incurred by resistance, even though precise quantitative values cannot be assigned to either. Moreover, such questions are, in principle, no different from those we address in our ordinary, less grandiose moral decision-making, when we are equally obliged to weigh up the incommensurable and uncertain outcomes of our actions. The difficulty is that in this case the problems are writ large and that, as I say, must inevitably give us pause. But, however daunting and difficult, an attempt to answer such questions is surely no more than the minimum requirement that rationality demands. Nor can this requirement be evaded by a simple judgement that war is never justified. For that judgement, if it is rationally founded, must itself be the conclusion of a similar calculation, albeit attempted on an immensely ambitious scale and seeking to predetermine the outcome for all possible cases. Such questions have, therefore, to be asked and the answers given may sometimes be surprising. The Second World War is judged generally to have been a just war for the Allies (despite some serious lapses) in which the overall suffering was not disproportionate to the good achieved in averting the Third Reich. And yet well over 50 million people lost their lives in the course of the war.

So much for the requirements that need to be met before a nation may legitimately resort to war. But even if all these conditions have been met, the just war doctrine insists that for a war to be just it has also to be conducted justly. To these criteria of the *jus in bello* we now turn.

The first condition for the just conduct of a war repeats the requirements of proportionality. As we have seen, to satisfy the *jus ad bellum*, this principle needs to be applied prior to the resort to war and the resulting balance sheet, relating the overall good aimed at by the war to the harm, needs to be regularly checked and rechecked during the course of the war to ensure its continued validity. This regular updating of the overall balance sheet does, of course, help to ameliorate the difficulties encountered in its construction prior to the war. If the balance of profit and loss looks very different, once the war has started, from how it did prior to hostilities it is incumbent upon a rational leader to reappraise the decision whether to continue the war. (One of the many criticisms of Allied policy in the First World War was precisely that the grisly attrition of the trenches did not occasion such a reappraisal.) But in addition to this, the just war theory requires that, to satisfy the *jus in bello*, the principle of proportion should be applied to each individual use of violence during the war. Thus, before any military operation is undertaken, an assessment should be made as to whether the harm likely to be caused is proportionate to the good aimed at by the specific operation.

This second application of the principle is sometimes faulted on the grounds that it is too permissive. It appears to license whatever conduces to the end of victory and thus at best 'rules out only purposeless or wanton violence':[17] a useful achievement, but no great moral gain. But this criticism overlooks the different levels at which the judgement of proportionality is to be made. A strategic decision is concerned, in Basil Liddell Hart's definition, with 'distributing and applying military means to fulfil *ends of policy*'[18] and those ends of policy are, as we have seen, constrained by the just cause for the sake of which the war is being conducted. Thus, at the highest military/political levels, an assessment of the justification for a strategic military decision would need to take into account not just its conduciveness to victory but the moral benefits to be secured by such victory. To the extent that the latter are in doubt, so will the amount of harm permitted be reduced: a point well emphasised by the US Catholic bishops' category of comparative justice. Indeed, in the case of a manifestly unjust war (for example, an act of naked aggression against a neighbouring country), the application of the principle at this level would rule out any use of violence since, *ex hypothesi*, there would no good against which the harm could be balanced.

This interpretation of the principle might then appear overrestrictive since it would appear to rule out the possibility of the just conduct of an unjust war: of which Rommel's behaviour in the Second World War is sometimes cited as an outstanding example. (Rommel, for example, refused to implement an order in 1942 from Hitler that enemy prisoners should be shot.) But this criticism is also based on a confusion between the levels of responsibility at which the principle is applied. At the highest politico-military levels, the principal agents in a war of aggression may indeed be unable legitimately to use the principle to justify any military action. But military commanders further away from the centre of politico-military decision-making, still more their junior colleagues in the field, cannot necessarily be held responsible for the unjust resort to war. These agents are, however, still required to apply the principle of proportion to their actions and thus charged to ensure that the harm they may thereby cause is not disproportionate to the specific benefits to be secured by their tactical military operations. For this reason, the Nuremberg tribunal rejected the argument that all military actions undertaken by the German armed forces were war crimes because carried out in pursuit of an aggressive war. Moreover, the converse also applies: military commanders fighting a just war can still be blamed for acts undertaken which cause harm disproportionate to the objectives aimed at by their operations.

Once the distinction is made between the various levels at which the principle of proportion needs to be applied, it is clear that it has rather more substance than is sometimes assumed. It may, however, still be felt that it can license too much and, indeed, it is precisely to ensure that this is not so that the just war theory supplements this principle with that of non-combatant immunity or, as it is also known, the principle of discrimination. To this principle we therefore now turn.

This principle, as usually enunciated, forbids direct attacks on non-combatants and non-military targets. But since killing any human being is at least, prima facie, a moral wrong, why should such a distinction be drawn between non-combatants and combatants? Surely the violent death of a young soldier, himself perhaps a reluctant conscript, is as much a moral tragedy as the death of a civilian? In either case, his hopes and plans for his life are prematurely terminated; in either case, the grief of family and friends will be no less acute. An answer frequently given within the just war tradition to this question is based on an analogy between war and judicial punishment. Just as within a state, the authorities may punish, if necessary by the death penalty, those guilty of subverting the order and tranquillity of the state, so a state has the right to take the life of those guilty of seeking its overthrow from without by external aggression. In Aquinas's words, quoting

St Paul, the political authorities are 'God's agents of punishment, for retribution of the offender'.[19] External aggressors are thus punished because they are guilty: the prohibition on killing the innocent remains intact.

There are considerable difficulties both with the general analogy between war and punishment and, more particularly, with the equation of combatants with the guilty deserving of punishment and of non-combatants with the morally blameless. If we assume that the offence deserving of punishment is the unjust resort to war, those guilty of this are likely to include non-combatants, especially the political leaders, while most combatants — the ordinary soldiers, sailors and airmen — are unlikely personally to have had any responsibility for or influence over the initial decision to resort to war. This is so, moreover, even if they are volunteers, still more the reluctant conscripts that comprise the bulk of modern armies. It might be tempting to seek to preserve the distinction by arguing that the ordinary combatants, even if not guilty of starting the war, are still guilty of its continued prosecution — for they could always refuse to fight. But even if we may reasonably require soldiers to refuse to fight in exceptional circumstances, for example if their orders are manifestly unlawful, this is not our normal expectation and the application of the concept of guilt in these circumstances still seems very strained. Ordinary members of the armed forces are as unlikely to have any influence over, or responsibility for, the decision whether to continue a war, as they had over its inception. They will not normally be privy to the strategic discussions of their military superiors and political masters which determine such matters.

Thus, it does not seem plausible to seek to justify the distinction between non-combatants and combatants in terms of their respective moral innocence and guilt. A better foundation for the distinction rests rather on the original meaning of innocent, i.e. non *nocent* or harming: what matters is, in Paul Ramsey's formulation, the 'degrees of actual participation in hostile force'.[20] If — as the just war theory claims — war can be justified to stop harm being done (for example, the invasion of a country by an external aggressor), then the use of proportionate force against those doing the harm must also be conceded: for how else normally can the harm be stopped? Those engaged in doing or threatening the harm will, of course, usually be the combatants and those not so engaged, the non-combatants. It is thus to prevent harm being done that the use of force against combatants is permitted. It is permissible to use proportionate violence against soldiers because they are prosecuting the war, not because they are guilty of so doing. The moral distinction between non-combatants and combatants rests simply on the question of who is doing the harm — who is *nocent* — regardless of their personal moral guilt or innocence.

Even this distinction might be faulted on the grounds that in a modern total war nearly every member of society is involved in some way in contributing to the war effort and could thus be regarded as contributing to the harm. But such an objection would be mistaken, for it ignores the substantial difference that still remains as to the degree of involvement. Certainly, some non-combatants (politicians, workers in munitions factories) may be held to contribute directly to the war effort and thus not be immune from attack. But the majority of the civilian population can be considered to constitute a direct threat of harm only in the most tenuous and ultimately specious sense. Thus, despite the inevitable grey areas, a clear distinction can be drawn and morally justified. As the US Catholic bishops say:

> Plainly . . . not even by the broadest definition can one naturally consider combatants entire classes of human beings such as school children, hospital patients, the elderly, the ill, the average industrial worker producing goods not directly related to military purposes, farmers and many others.[21]

The distinction presupposed by the principle of non-combatant immunity can thus be justified. But it remains for consideration quite what is the scope of the principle and whether it should be regarded as absolute, admitting of no exception. This is a complex but crucial issue to which I shall devote the next chapter.

3 THE JUST WAR TRADITION II: NON-COMBATANT IMMUNITY AND DOUBLE EFFECT

The principle of non-combatant immunity, in its usual modern formulation, prohibits any direct military attack on non-combatants. In most modern applications of the just war theory the principle is afforded considerable prominence and is normally deemed to be an absolute principle, admitting of no exception. By contrast, within the just war tradition the principle was, historically, given much less prominence — not appearing in recognisable modern form in the earlier authors such as Augustine, Gratian and Aquinas. When it does appear in the sixteenth- and seventeenth-century authors, derived from the confluence of chivalric tradition and the piecemeal immunities granted in canon law to certain classes of citizenry, such as pilgrims, clerics and peasants tilling the soil, it is not usually regarded as absolute.[1]

In view of the absolute status recently accorded the principle, it might appear that modern proponents of the just war theory would be obliged to conclude that most wars past and present have been unjust since they have — particularly in the experience of this century — caused very substantial civilian casualties. That this conclusion has not normally been drawn owes much to the use that has also been made of the Catholic doctrine of double effect which defines somewhat narrowly what is to count as a 'direct attack'. The principle of double effect has thus enabled modern just war theorists to soften the otherwise unyielding rigour of the absolute status accorded non-combatant immunity.

The doctrine of double effect is traceable to Aquinas but was fully developed by the sixteenth-century theologians of Salamance.[2] In its modern form, the doctrine states that it is normally permissible to carry out acts with foreseen morally bad consequences provided:

(i) the act (which must itself be at least morally neutral) is undertaken for the sake of good effects;

(ii) the bad consequences are merely foreseen and not intended, i.e. they are wanted neither as the means to the result aimed at nor as

the end itself;
(iii) the bad consequences are not disproportionate to the good
aimed at.

On this basis, a military operation resulting in civilian casualties
would not count as a direct attack on non-combatants, if the
civilian casualties are not wanted as either the means or end of the
action, but are merely its foreseen side effects. It may thus be
permissible to bomb a munitions factory, even though it is foreseen
that civilians living nearby will be killed, provided their deaths are
not chosen as either the means or end of the action, and provided
the harm thereby caused is not disproportionate to the benefits
aimed at.

Double effect has a much wider application than simply within
the just war theory, for it can be used to soften the rigours of any
absolute ethical principle. Double effect has thus a very considerable attraction for moral absolutists, i.e. those who hold that
some fundamental moral principles are absolutely binding. It
appears to offer a way of reconciling this belief with our ordinary
moral judgements that some acts which breach such moral
principles may still be morally licit. Double effect achieves this
remarkable feat by arguing that such breaches are more apparent
than real: the absolute moral principles remain intact. Professor
Anscombe says:

> The distinction between the intended and the merely foreseen
> effects of a voluntary action is indeed absolutely crucial to
> Christian ethics. For Christianity forbids a number of things as
> being bad in themselves but if I am answerable for the foreseen
> consequences of an action or refusal, as much as for the action
> itself, then the prohibitions will break down.[3]

Absolutism is thus a normal presumption of the principle of
double effect. If absolutism were false, much of the need for the
principle would disappear. But double effect does not necessarily
presuppose absolutism. It might be held to mark an important
moral distiction, even if absolutism were rejected. I shall,
therefore, initially examine the principle on its own merits before
addressing some of the wider issues of absolutism and, in
particular, the alleged absolute status of non-combatant immunity.
The principle of double effect logically presupposes that: (i) a

clear distinction can be drawn between what is intended and what is merely foreseen; (ii) this distinction is morally important. The doctrine also presupposes the moral relevance of proportionality. This is important, although sometimes neglected in modern secular philosophical discussion of double effect, since it would still rule out as morally permissible acts whose foreseen harmful side effects are judged disproportionate to the good aimed at. With the principle of proportionality I have no quarrel. My present concern is therefore with the other presuppositions of double effect.

In some cases a clear distinction between what is foreseen and what is intended both can and needs to be made. Two examples will help illustrate this. First, suppose a man gets up in the middle of the night to drink a glass of water foreseeing that this will awake the baby.[4] He does not want to wake the baby either as an end or a means of his action — indeed, he would rather the baby stayed asleep. It thus seems plausible to say that he merely foresees that he will awake the baby but does not intend this.

The next example, drawn from English law, is the case of *Regina v Desmond, Barrett and others*.[5] In 1868 the accused attempted to free two Fenians by blowing up the wall of Clerkenwell prison and, in consequence, killed some people living nearby. They may have foreseen their deaths but did not intend them in the sense of choosing them as the means or end of their action. Indeed, if they had not died, their intention of freeing the Fenians by blowing a hole in the prison wall would still have been fulfilled. In discussing this case, Hart contrasts what actually happened with the hypothetical supposition that Barrett and his Fenian colleagues had deliberately shot one of the prison warders in order to secure the keys to the prison gate. That death would have been intended as a means to their end.

Why should the distinction between what is foreseen and what is intended as the end or means of an action have any moral relevance? Part of the answer is that it is a fundamental presumption of any moral system that one should not pursue as the end of one's action outcomes that are morally harmful: morality is, after all, concerned with promoting good and reducing harm. The moral relevance of this part of the distinction seems thus uncontentious. What requires more explanation is the basis of the moral distinction drawn between those consequences of an action which are the chosen means to secure a result and those that are its foreseen side effects. I shall consider two possible reasons for the moral relevance of this distinction.

First, it would, in general, seem easier for a harmful side effect to be judged proportionate to a good aimed at than a chosen means. This is because where the side effect is less than certain, one can discount the harm according to its uncertainty: for the expected disbenefit is a function of both the harm caused and the probability of its occurrence. But this discounting cannot be done with a harmful chosen means to secure the good end. If the harm of the means is uncertain, so is the good of the end: for it is through that means that the end is to be brought about.

Secondly, it may be suggested that the distinction reflects the considerable importance we attach, in our moral evaluation of actions, to the beliefs and attitudes that we attribute to the agents. This is illustrated by Strawson's example:

> If someone treads on my hand accidentally, while trying to help me, the pain may be no less acute than if he treads on it in contemptuous disregard for my existence or with a malevolent wish to injure me. But I shall generally feel in the second case a kind and degree of resentment that I shall not feel in the first.[6]

There thus appears some basis for the distinction between what is foreseen and what is intended and for its moral relevance. But in other cases the distinction and its moral relevance appear less clear, as illustrated by the following cases of abortion much discussed in the philosophical literature.[7] In the first case a pregnant woman suffering from cancer will die unless the surgeon removes her womb with the foetus inside, which will then die. In the second case the woman will die unless a craniotomy is performed, crushing the skull of the unborn foetus. In the third case the mother's life can only be saved by killing the foetus within the womb by altering the chemical composition of the amniotic fluid with the injection of a saline solution. Let us suppose — in order to keep the examples parallel and to avoid difficult questions about the relative value of the lives of mother and foetus — that in all three cases, if the operation is carried out, the mother will live but the foetus will die; if the operation is not carried out, both mother and foetus will die.[8]

Traditional Catholic doctrine, relying on the principle of double effect, draws a crucial moral distinction between the first case and the other two. In the first case, the death of the foetus is regarded as merely the unintended side effect of the hysterectomy, willed neither as an end nor a means; in the second case, crushing the baby's skull is considered so intimately connected with the baby's death that the surgeon must be assumed to intend the death of the baby as the means of saving the mother's life, as he must also be assumed to do in the third case. These distinctions, taken together with an absolute prohibition on intentionally taking innocent life, entail that only in the first case is abortion permitted; in the second and third cases the mother and baby should be allowed to die, even though in none of the cases is the death of the foetus the end of the action.

At first glance, the distinction thus drawn between what is merely a foreseen side effect and an intended effect appears plausible. But the more one reflects on the cases, the more the dividing line between a side effect and an intended effect appears indistinct and arbitrary. It would thus seem possible to argue plausibly that in all three cases the death of the foetus is intended, for in all three cases the death is within the surgeon's control, and so closely connected with his chosen means of saving the mother's life as to be reasonably regarded as part of that means. Alternatively, it has been argued, although perhaps less plausibly, that at least in the first two cases the death of the foetus is unintended: the surgeon's chosen means of saving the mother's life is simply the removal of the foetus whether by hysterectomy or craniotomy: its consequent death is just a side effect. How are we to choose between these alternative descriptions?

At this point, one might try to preserve the distinction between what is foreseen and intended by introducing the concept of consent. Where a consequence is deemed the inevitable or very likely result of one's act and it is within one's control whether or not that consequence happens, then the agent who none the less does the act must at least have been willing that the consequence should happen, must have consented to its occurrence, even if he does not choose it as either the means or end of his action. Thus it might be argued that in all three cases, if the operation is performed, the surgeon consented to the death of the foetus but only in the second and third cases did he also intend it. Only in the first case is the operation therefore permitted. The crucial distinction is now between what is intended (deliberately chosen as a means) and what is foreseen and consented to.

But what now seems questionable is whether so fine a distinction as that between consent and intention can provide the basis for such a major moral distinction. In all three cases the mother and foetus will die unless the operation is performed; in no case is the death of the foetus aimed at for its own sake; but in only one case is the operation permitted since, in that case, the death of the foetus, although consented to, is not intended. When the consequences at stake are so important, can so much moral weight be placed on so delicate a distinction as that between consent and intention?

At least in the case of murder, the English law apparently thinks not. In the *Desmond* case quoted earlier, Lord Coleridge concluded that it is murder, 'if a man did an act not with the purpose of taking life but with the knowledge or belief that life was likely to be sacrificed by it'.[9] This is, of course, not conclusive both because the exact status of English law in this area (and the significance of Lord Coleridge's judgement) is open to dispute[10] and because, in any case, legal distinctions do not necessarily always correspond to moral ones.

Let us, therefore, reconsider the hand-crushing example introduced earlier to illustrate the importance which mental attitudes can have in our moral evaluation. Let us suppose that:

(i) the agent intended to crush my hand;
(ii) the agent foresaw that my hand would inevitably be crushed as the result of what he was doing and was, none the less, willing that it should be crushed;
(iii) the agent crushed my hand accidentally (he was, for example, pushed or slipped).

The distinction between variant (iii) (where the hand-crushing was not within his control or consented to) and variants (i) and (ii) (where it was within his control and consented to) is clear and important. But the moral relevance of the distinction between (i) and (ii) appears, by contrast, more slender: in either case I should feel a not dissimilar degree of resentment. The crucial moral distinction thus appears to be between whether or not the hand-crushing was within his control and yet he was willing that it should happen, rather than the much finer distinction between whether he intended it or merely foresaw and consented to it. Likewise, in the abortion cases, the similarities between the cases would appear to matter more than the dissimilarities: in all three cases the death of the foetus is within the agent's control but is consented to, as an unavoidable concomitant of saving the mother's life, which would otherwise be lost, together with that of the foetus.

The discussion thus far suggests that, at least in cases where morally significant consequences are judged inevitable, double effect places more weight than it can bear on the simple distinction between foresight and intention. For in such cases the distinction appears too arbitrary or, even where it can still be clearly drawn, too tenuous to base a major difference in moral evaluation. Nor can one rescue the moral relevance of the distinction by the argument that harmful side effects can be more readily discounted according to their uncertainty than chosen means: for — *ex hypothesi* — both are equally certain. Rather, what seems to matter more to the moral evaluation of such cases is whether or not the consequences were within the agent's control and he was, none the less, willing that they should happen.

This way of making the distinction also appears more helpful in explaining the basis of our moral judgements even in cases where the foreseen consequences are not certain. To explore this let us consider the following incident from Frank Richards's memoir of the First World War:

> When bombing dug-outs, it was always wise to throw bombs into them first and have a look around after. But we had to be careful in this village as there were civilians in some of the cellars. We shouted down to them to make sure. Another man and I shouted down one cellar twice and receiving no reply were just about to pull the pins out of our bombs when we heard a woman's voice and a young lady came up the cellar steps . . . She and the members of her family . . . had not left [the cellar] for some days. They guessed an attack was being made and when we first shouted down had been too frightened to answer. If the young lady had not cried out when she did, we would have innocently murdered them all.[11]

Let us now consider three possible variations on what actually happened, in each of which Richards's sole aim remains that of clearing the cellars of enemy soldiers:

(i) Reports from captured German soldiers have attested that civilians have been evacuated from the area. The reports are judged trustworthy. Richards has thus good reason to believe that there are no civilians sheltering in the cellars. He lobs in the bomb without warning. The young lady and family, who had unfortunately not been evacuated, are killed.

(ii) Richards has good reason to believe that civilians are sheltering in some of the cellars. He therefore takes the avoiding action as described. But — as very nearly happened in Richards's account — the young lady fails to respond. She and her family are killed.

(iii) Richards has good reason to believe that civilians are sheltering in the cellars. He none the less lobs in the bomb without warning. The young lady and her family are killed.

Richards's action in the first two cases appears justifiable, but not in case (iii). What is the basis for the felt moral difference? This cannot be explained by the distinction between foresight and intention, since in all three cases the deaths are unintended. Part of the answer undoubtedly rests on the fact that, whereas in case (i), where the risk of civilian casualties is believed to be very low, and in case (ii), where the risk is higher but steps have now been taken to reduce it, it seems easier to judge the action consistent with the principle of proportion than in case (iii). In view of the low risk, the expected disbenefit of civilian casualties (a function, as noted earlier, of both the harm and the probability of its occurrence) may more readily be judged not disproportionate to the benefit aimed at. But in case (iii), there is little if any room for such discounting.

This is, undoubtedly, an important part of our moral evaluation. But other factors are also relevant. Part of our condemnation of variant (iii) surely also rests on the fact that in this example, even if the deaths are unintended, their occurrence is within Richards's control and yet he is willing that they should happen. But in variant (i), where the risk is judged small, and in case (ii), where efforts have been made to reduce the risk, the civilian casualties are not so directly within his control (for example, in variant (ii) the young lady's ignoring the warning is also clearly relevant) and he could reasonably claim that he had not consented to the deaths, even though he had been prepared to accept some small risk of their occurrence.

I therefore conclude that double effect, as traditionally formulated, appears to draw the moral dividing line at the wrong place: the crucial moral distinction is not between those consequences that are intended and those that are foreseen, but rather depends on the extent to which the consequences are held to be within the agent's control and consented to by him, as evidenced — *inter alia* — by his belief about the likelihood of their occurrence and action taken, where appropriate, to reduce this. This formulation helps explain why intentions are important to a moral assessment, since an agent must regard the intended consequences of his action as, at least to some extent, within his control (a point further explored in Chapter 6) and, if they are intended, they are *a fortiori* consented to. But it blocks off the use of lack of intention as too ready an excuse to evade moral responsibility. The formulation also has important implications for the alleged absolute status of the prohibition on killing the innocent and, hence, on the principle of non-combatant immunity.

One of the attractions of the principle of double effect in its traditional version was that it appeared to offer a way of reconciling such an absolutist belief with at least some of our ordinary moral judgements in cases such as the abortion examples discussed earlier. It thus helped to render such an absolutist stance more plausible. But the necessary modifications to the principle which I have proposed substantially reduce its ability to accomplish this feat. For in all three abortion variants the modified double effect principle would discern no significant moral difference: in all three cases the death of the foetus is within the surgeon's control and consented to by him. If the taking of life in such circumstances is always morally wrong (and the foetus can hardly plausibly be regarded as a 'combatant'),[12] the operation should not be performed. The moral absolutist must therefore, presumably, conclude that it is morally better to allow the mother and foetus to die rather than bring about the death of the foetus — a conclusion which appears morally perverse. It places enormous moral weight upon the distinction between what we do and what we allow to happen: between our acts and omissions. But without the underpinning of the traditional version of double effect, it is difficult to see how the act/omission distinction can bear such weight.

This is not to deny that an important moral distinction can be drawn between some acts and omissions, even where the consequences are identical: not least since omissions may, rather more often than acts, be the result of negligence and thoughtlessness, with the resulting consequences neither foreseen nor consented to: 'I hadn't realised', 'I didn't think', 'I didn't know' are typical excuses in such cases. But where an act or omission has identical consequences, equally within the agent's control and consented to by him, the moral distinction becomes tenuous. The hospital ward orderly, who has inveigled an elderly, terminally ill patient to bequeath him all her money, hardly seems less culpable if he deliberately fails to switch her life support machine on (an omission) than if he deliberately switches it off (an act). In such circumstances, it seems implausible to claim that the act is — of its intrinsic nature — somehow worse than the omission. Still less does this appear plausible where, as in the abortion cases, the result of the omission is very much worse than that of the act. The death of the mother and foetus would not be the result of negligence or inadvertence on the surgeon's part. On the contrary, the choice with which he is faced is whether deliberately to save the mother and cause the death of the foetus or deliberately to allow both to die: either outcome is equally within his control, either outcome, if it comes about, would have been consented to by him. The effective moral choice with which he is presented in all three examples is that between saving one life at the cost of one death or failing to prevent two deaths: an unenviable choice but one where, to me, the answer seems clear. The surgeon should save the mother's life. It is, thus, perhaps for good reason that one of the confessions in the Anglican Book of Common Prayer seeks forgiveness both for 'the evil we have done' and 'the good we have not done'.

Without the benefit of the traditional double effect doctrine, the absolutist cannot claim that the breach of the absolute prohibition on killing innocents is only apparent rather than real. He is thus obliged to face up to the choice of either giving up the absolute status of this principle or clinging on to it, regardless of the moral cost in terms of the suffering and unnecessary deaths that it involves. Moreover, as the following examples show, this dilemma would still have to be faced even if the traditional formulation of double effect had not been abandoned. The first example is one discussed by Bernard Williams:

Jim finds himself in the central square of a small South American town. Tied up against the wall are a row of twenty Indians, most terrified, a few defiant, in front of them several men in uniform. A heavy man in a sweat-stained khaki shirt turns out to be the captain in charge and, after a good deal of questioning of Jim, which establishes that he got there by accident while on a botanical expedition, explains that the Indians are a random group of the inhabitants who, after recent acts of protest against the government, are just about to be killed to remind other possible protestors of the advantages of not protesting. However, since Jim is an honoured visitor from another land, the captain is happy to offer him a guest's privilege of killing one of the Indians himself. If Jim accepts, then as a special mark of the occasion, the other Indians will be let off. Of course, if Jim refuses, then there is no special occasion and Pedro here will do what he was about to do when Jim arrived, and kill them all . . . The men against the wall, and the other villagers, understand the situation, and are obviously begging him to accept. What should he do?[13]

It seems clear to me that, faced with such an appalling moral choice, Jim should shoot one of the Indians in order to save the lives of 19. But if he does so, he surely intends the death and does not merely foresee it as a likely consequence of his action. On the contrary, it is the means he chooses to save the lives of the remaining 19. Traditional double effect, even if valid, could have no application in this case. Nor would it appear to help in the parallel case, discussed by Paskins and Dockrill, of the 'innocent shield'.[14] In this example, a terrorist has seized a hostage and is about to spray machine-gun bullets into a crowd of innocent by-standers. The crowd cannot be evacuated; a police marksman can only stop the gunman by shooting him through the hostage, in a way that he knows will kill the hostage. Once again, it seems clear that the hostage should be shot if this is the only way to save the lives of many innocents. But once again, it seems clear that, if so, the hostage's death would be intended: it would be the chosen means of killing the terrorist so as to prevent him machine-gunning the crowd. Traditional double effect would therefore not have helped to transform such a morally permissible breach of an absolute rule into a merely apparent breach.

It might be argued against this that the death of the hostage is not intended since it is not his death but the passage of the bullet through his body that is the chosen means of killing the terrorist. If the hostage survives, the police will be delighted. But since, ex hypothesi, shooting the hostage will kill him, it seems as implausible to distinguish between the two acts (causing a bullet to pass through his vital organs and killing him) as to make a distinction in the craniotomy case between killing the foetus and crushing his skull. Moreover, such linguistic manoeuvres are not available in the case of Jim and the Indians. The death of one Indian is precisely the chosen means to save the others: without his death, the others will not be saved. Nor will it help to argue that, if things had turned out differently from how we have supposed — for example, if some means of escape had been available to the hostage — the police marksman would not then have sought to kill him. This is, of course, so since the death of the hostage is not the end of his action and is only his chosen means *faute de mieux*. But from this it no more follows that he does not intend to kill the hostage, given the unenviable situation with which he is faced, than would Barrett's claim, in the hypothetical case earlier discussed, that he did not intend to shoot the prison warder because he would not have done so had the keys been left in the prison gate. Perhaps that is true but, since the keys were not thus left, he chose the death of the warder as the means to secure the keys and hence his escape. Unfortunately, we have to act and to frame our intentions in the world as we find it, where sometimes the only means to save many innocent lives is deliberately to take an innocent life.

The absolutist might still argue that the intention to breach the moral rule belongs not to Jim or the police marksman but rather to the South American captain or the terrorist. It is they, after all, who have placed the agent in such a morally intolerable position. But although the latter is true and explains why we judge the terrorist or South American captain morally culpable, it does not enable Jim or the police marksman to evade the agonising moral choice with which they are faced: for it is still true that, if they do not act, many lives will be lost. Moreover, such moral dilemmas can arise without there being another agent to whom blame can be attributed. This is illustrated by the fat man and the cave.[15] The fat man has been leading a party of 20 schoolchildren on a pot-holing expedition. Unfortunately, the fat man has got stuck in the mouth of a subterranean cave. Oxygen is running out. The rescue party arrives. They quickly discover that the only way they can save the children is by blowing up the fat man. Again, a cruel dilemma, but this time there is no wicked captain or terrorist who can be blamed for the dilemma.

What these examples suggest is that situations can arise in which there is a clash between the moral requirement to prevent evil, if it is readily in our power to do so, and the duty to refrain from killing the innocent; and that, if the only way to prevent a much greater harm, such as the slaughter of many innocents, is to take a life, this may be morally licit and even right. Moreover, traditional double effect cannot plausibly be invoked to disguise the fact that the alleged absolute moral rule has thereby been breached. But the absolutist may still seek to evade this conclusion on two further grounds.

First, he may concede that it is right to choose to do the lesser evil where I have no choice but to do one of two acts either of which involves harm, but may argue that this does not justify my doing a bad act to prevent others, such as the terrorist, doing something worse. For the latter is not a choice between two evils but choosing evil that good may come and the end does not justify the means. But this argument presupposes the absolute moral distinction between acts and omission which we have already questioned. For it is to argue that to fail to prevent very great harm being done to others, which it is readily within my power to prevent, is better simply because it is an omission than to perform an act which, though involving harm, is, *ex hypothesi*, less harmful. And this seems deeply implausible. Nor need recognition of this implausibility commit us to the ethically dubious proposition that where our end is the prevention of evil this justifies *any* means, for that is not so. Quite apart from the requirement that the means should be proportionate to the end, if the end can be secured by either A or B where A is harmful and B indifferent, one should choose B. But if a very great harm can only be prevented by A and if the good thereby achieved clearly and decisively outweighs the harm, it may be permissible to do A.

Secondly, the absolutist may argue that if some breaches of moral rules are deemed permissible, it will be impossible to hold the line. The floodgates will be open to all kinds of morally dubious practices. These might include the judicial execution of an innocent scapegoat to prevent a riot in which many more will be killed or the killing off of a hospital patient so that his organs and vital parts can be used in spare part surgery to save the lives of other patients.

But this is moral defeatism. From the fact that it may, in exceptional cases such as those considered earlier, be morally licit to take life, it pre-eminently does not follow that such exceptions should become the rule. In view of the very strong moral presumption against killing the innocent and the acknowledged imperfections of human reasoning in discerning when breaches may be justified, there are very good reasons for holding firm to the prohibition and only allowing it to be overriden, if at all, if this is the only way to prevent much greater harm and the good thereby achieved clearly and decisively outweighs the harm: the trading of one life for another for marginal moral advantage remains forbidden. But in the moral horror comic examples usually cited, it is very difficult to see how these conditions can be met: on the contrary, the moral harm seems far to outweigh any good. This is readily seen in the judicial scapegoat or spare parts surgery cases by considering not only the moral harm perpetrated against those innocents but also the quite appalling effects which the condoning, still more licensing, of such practices would have more generally, not least on public confidence in the judicial and medical systems. We should, for example, surely be very reluctant — despite the suffering thereby caused — to entrust ailing grandparents, children or even ourselves to the tender mercies of a medical system that we knew might treat them (or us) not as patients to be cured but as timely repositories of spare organs for transplant operations. The counter-supposition, that such practices could be kept secret, is, by the nature of the examples, highly implausible and could be achieved, if at all, only by conceding to public officials the right to behave in so duplicitous and manipulative a manner as to subvert the foundations of a free and open society.

The relevant distinction between the kind of principled consequentialism at which we have thus arrived and absolutism is not that for the absolutist some acts are morally impermissible, whereas for the principled consequentialist 'anything goes'. The distinction rests rather on the question of what facts are to be taken into account in assessing the moral status of an act and, in particular, the principled consequentialist's insistence that sometimes the consequences of the performance or non-performance of an act may be as important or even more important than its internal quality. The principled consequentialist shares with the absolutist acceptance of the presumption against breaching such a fundamental moral rule as the prohibition on killing the innocent and the very strong reasons for, in general, holding fast to the principle. But he parts company from the absolutist in holding that exceptionally the consequences of not breaching the rule may be so bad as to override that presumption and that in such cases it would be wrong to focus attention on the internal quality of the act (e.g. intentionally killing an innocent) to the neglect of the consequences (e.g. saving the lives of many more innocents). But equally if — as in the moral horror comic examples just considered — the balance of harm outweighs the good, or even if the probable moral profit looks merely marginal, the act — and any act of the same kind as regards its internal quality and consequences — would remain forbidden. The criticism of the absolutist in this respect is not that he renders certain acts absolutely wrong but that in so doing he defines too narrowly what is to be included in the moral reckoning and hence over-simplifies the complexities of our moral predicament.

Moreover, even if one concedes that, in exceptional cases, it may be morally permissible to breach a moral rule, it does not follow from anything I have argued that the breach does not still involve some moral harm: not, of course, in the sense that it is the wrong thing to do, but in the sense that, if it is done, moral harm will result. One can, of course (and some utilitarians do), define right and wrong in such a way that the right thing to do is thereby erased of any moral blemish. But the justification for such definitional manoeuvres seems somewhat suspect. For, however much one may believe that it is morally permissible and even right to breach a moral rule in such agonising cases, moral harm will still — in a very real sense — have been done: a life will have been terminated. It is precisely from this fact that the moral agony derives.

But neither the utilitarian who chooses to define right and wrong in such a way as to obscure this fact nor the absolutist who pretends that fundamental moral principles never conflict can adequately account for the moral dilemma. The absolutist may be correct to insist that, if the moral rule is breached, moral harm is done, but he is mistaken in neglecting the even graver moral objections to not breaching the rule. The utilitarian is correct to insist that a breach of the rule may exceptionally be justified but mistaken to ignore the moral harm that is still done. For without both sides of the picture the source of the moral dilemma is left obscure. Both parties, arguing from opposite ends of the moral spectrum, thus seem guilty of a gross moral naïveté: the supposition that our moral choices are always between good and evil. But it is a regrettable fact, which not even the ingenuities of double effect can finally obscure, that, in the post-lapsarian world we actually inhabit, our moral choices may sometimes be not between good and evil but between evil and evil. And in such cases, as I have tried to show, it may be morally permissible, indeed morally right, to choose the lesser of the two evils with which we are presented.

In the light of the preceding discussion, let us now revert to the principle of non-combatant immunity. Since the general prohibition on killing the innocent, from which this principle is derived, cannot be deemed to admit of no exception, it seems clear that the absolute status recently accorded non-combatant immunity is mistaken. Although any breach of the principle will involve moral harm, such breaches may, exceptionally, be licit. Nor is this conclusion, I believe, inconsistent with the version of the just war theory presented in the last chapter. For I there argued that the permission to use proportionate force against combatants derives from the fact that, since combatants are those who are prosecuting the harm, this is usually the only way to prevent harm being done to one's fellow countrymen by an external aggressor. But if, in exceptional circumstances, the only way to prevent such harm is by military action which results in non-combatant casualties, this too — provided the harm thereby caused is not disproportionate — might be held permissible. As, however, with the more general prohibition on taking life, so with the principle of non-combatant immunity, there are very compelling reasons for licensing such breaches only exceptionally.

War, as has frequently been stressed, causes immense human suffering. The value of the principle of non-combatant immunity is that it provides a reasonably clear-cut and justifiable way of restricting that suffering. There are therefore very strong reasons for holding firm to the principle, particularly since — as stressed by the principle of comparative justice — those caught up in the heat and fury of battle are unlikely to be best placed to make a rational and unbiased assessment as to when an exception to the rule may be justified. They may be only too tempted to trade speculative gains, of perhaps doubtful moral value, for the very real and evident moral disbenefit of non-combatant casualties. None the less, if, after taking all these and other imperfections of human reasoning into account, it remains true that military action causing non-combatant casualties is the only way to prevent a very great harm and where the good thereby achieved will clearly and decisively outweigh the harm, such action — however morally repugnant — may be licit.

The formulation of the principle of non-combatant immunity with which we started forbade any direct attack upon non-combatants. This formulation would appear, on the one hand, too strict since such action might, on occasion, be morally licit, but, on the other hand, too lax since it makes the mere lack of intention too readily available as an excuse. The balance required is perhaps best encapsulated in the dictum of the seventeenth-century Puritan divine William Ames: 'Charity and Aequity doth require that the Warre be so managed as the innocent may bee as little damnified as possible.'[16] The requirement thus becomes to minimise non-combatant casualties as far as possible. This formulation seems helpful since it encapsulates the very strong moral presumption against military action that causes the deaths of non-combatants, whether intentionally or as the foreseen inevitable consequence, while not excluding altogether its possible legitimacy. It also helpfully stresses that even where such casualties are not certain, every reasonable effort should be made to minimise the risk of their occurrence. On this basis, military action involving risk to civilians is permissible where the risk is judged small or where efforts have been made to reduce the risk; where the military action would inevitably cause non-combatant deaths, even if these are unintended, it is permissible if and only if there is very good reason to believe that this is the only way to avoid a very great harm and that the good thereby achieved would clearly and decisively outweigh the harm. These requirements are, moreover, additional to and impose further constraint on those demanded by the principle of proportion which has also to be satisfied: where non-combatants are involved, a mere balance of probable moral advantage is not enough.

To see quite what would and would not be licensed by the principle of non-combatant immunity, as thus qualified, let us consider the following three hypothetical cases of conventional aerial bombing during the Second World War:

(a) A German munitions factory, situated away from major residential areas, is attacked with precisely aimed bombs of relatively low explosive power.
(b) A German munitions factory, surrounded by residential areas whose residents do not work in the factory, is bombed with imprecisely aimed large bombs. Very substantial civilian casualties are known to be inevitable.
(c) The residential areas of a German city are themselves directly attacked: civilian casualties are expected to be of the same order as in case (b).

There are clearly morally relevant differences between each of these cases. But the crucial moral dividing line would, on the modified version of double effect that I have presented, appear to be between case (a) and the rest. Thus, even though only in case (c) are the deaths directly intended, in case (b) they are still within the agent's control and consented to. But in case (a), where efforts have been made to minimise civilian casualties — as evidenced by the choice of target, precision of aim and size of bomb — any resulting civilian casualties, provided they are not disproportionate to the good aimed at, could be regarded as the morally licit collateral effects of legitimate military action.

There is thus a clear presumption against the moral permissibility of cases (b) and (c). To assess whether, none the less, they might be morally justifiable, such episodes would need to be related more closely to their historical context within the course of the war and to the justifiability or otherwise, judged by the just war criteria, of the overall Allied policy of area bombing.

The Allies' area bombing campaign against Germany probably started with the attack on the city of Mannheim in December 1940, in reprisal for the German devastation of Coventry. Attacks, ostensibly aimed at industrial targets, but in practice, because of the lack of effective navigational aids, hitting cities fairly indiscriminately, continued throughout 1941. Early in 1942 the policy of aerial bombardment with the explicit objective of destroying the German people's capacity and will to make war was formally endorsed. City bombing then continued right up to the end of the war, albeit increasingly supplemented, particularly from 1944, by more accurate attacks — made possible by improved targeting techniques — on military and industrial assets. The German area bombing campaign culminated in the devastating attack on Dresden in February 1945 in which perhaps 60,000 people were killed.

Was the policy morally justifiable? For this to be so, given the very substantial non-combatant suffering caused, there would have had to be very good reason to suppose that such a bombing campaign was the only way to prevent a very great harm and that the good thereby achieved would clearly and decisively outweigh the harm. Let us consider if these conditions were satisfied.

The threat posed by Nazi aggression was certainly a great and, in the early years of the war, imminent evil. It is also arguable that in those early years, when Britain stood alone, following the collapse of France and the ejection of the British expeditionary force from the continent, area bombing (in the absence at that time of navigational and other aids to permit precision bombing) was the only means available to attempt to prevent the spread of Nazi aggression: as Churchill remarked in September 1940, 'The bombers alone provide the means of victory'.[17] But by the time area bombing got into full swing in 1942 this was no longer so. Churchill conceded this in July 1942:

> In the days when we were fighting alone, we answered the question: 'How are you going to win the war?' by saying: 'We will shatter Germany by bombing.' Since then the enormous injuries inflicted on the German Army and manpower by the Russians, and the accession of the manpower and munitions of the United States, have rendered other possibilities open.[18]

By 1942 not only had other possibilities thus appeared which ostensibly offered a way to defeat Hitler without the need for a policy deliberately aimed at maximising non-combatant casualties but the universal triumph of Nazism was no longer so overwhelmingly imminent. An immense burden of proof was therefore required of those who sought to justify area bombing to show that its continued prosecution was essential to avert the success of Nazism and that the massive and immediate non-combatant suffering caused was clearly and decisively outweighed by the good achieved.

In retrospect, it is doubtful whether such demands were met. The claim that area bombing alone could achieve victory at less cost to non-combatants than a full-scale land campaign fought on the heavily populated territory of Europe proved unfounded: for the latter was what finally achieved the overthrow of Hitler. Moreover, even the contribution that area bombing made to the overall combined Allied strategy for winning the European war was less than its advocates had supposed. Area bombing failed to break either the German people's will or their capacity to make war. Munitions production more than trebled during the period 1942–4: a far more effective contribution to the destruction of the German war-making capacity was made by the precision bombing of the last year of the war against military and related targets, particularly oil production and transportation facilities.

Such judgements are made with hindsight. But it is questionable whether even at the time there was very good reason to suppose that the good achieved by area bombing would be sufficient to over-ride the massive moral presumption against such a policy; and whether the weight of that presumption and, hence, of the need to prosecute the war, if at all possible, by alternative means was fully appreciated by those concerned with formulating the strategy.[19] The Blitz failed to break British morale and it is arguable that Hitler made a serious military error, which could have affected the outcome of the Battle of Britain, in switching to bombing British cities from bombing fighter production and key elements of fighter command. It was, thus, hardly self-evident that similar tactics would break German morale and, even if they did, there was a crucial failure to explain how damaged civilian morale was supposed to lead to lost production, when economic necessity and habit motivated the German workers otherwise, and, even more importantly, how it was supposed to induce the political changes required to end the fighting in a totalitarian society, from which all organised political opposition had been barred.

The bulk of the area bombing campaign (1942–5) would thus appear to fail to meet the criteria and stand condemned, while there are serious doubts over the justification of the campaign even in the early years of the war. In those years, however, when Britain stood alone and Nazi armies were everywhere victorious, I have no doubt that things looked very different. It may then, perhaps, have seemed not unreasonable to suppose that the area bombing campaign was both the only and an effective way of averting the imminent triumph of Nazism. I defer to historians to settle such matters, if they can. From a moral viewpoint what is important is that, even if area bombing in the early years of the war might have been morally justified, it would appear difficult so to justify the bulk of the campaign (from 1942 onwards). And this, I hope, helps illustrate the strict limits set by the principle of non-combatant immunity, even in the qualified form in which I have presented it.

This completes our survey of each of the conditions set by the just war theory. It has, I hope, helped show that the just war theory is not a fossilised deposit from the past of little more than anti-quarian interest. On the contrary, it is a living tradition enunciating valid moral principles for restricting the suffering caused by war. In view of the inevitability of such suffering if war occurs, it appears eminently reasonable that no war can be justified unless declared by a legitimate government, as a last resort, for the sake of a just cause and, only then, if the harm judged likely to result is not disproportionate to the good aimed at; and in the conduct of the war, proportion should be observed, as should the need to minimise non-combatant casualties.

Application of these principles to individual cases may be notoriously difficult. But the difficulties are inherent in the very nature of moral decision-making and do not in themselves invalidate the theory, any more than does the fact that the principles may be open to abuse by wilful and deceitful men. Nor should we be frightened by the fact of cultural pluralism into the adoption of an uncritical cultural and ethical relativism: the assumption that any society is as good as another, that there are no values left worth defending, that aggression is no worse than defence, that the justice in 'just cause' has been drained of all substantive content. The fact that many, perhaps most, wars fought in the past have been unjust does not detract from the truth that some have been just and that the fighting of a just war may be not merely morally permissible, it may — according to the just war theory — be a moral duty.

4 JUST WAR AND NUCLEAR WEAPONS: A PRELIMINARY ASSESSMENT

Our survey of the just war tradition in the last two chapters concluded that it provided a valid moral framework against which to assess modern warfare. In this chapter, I shall consider what are the particular moral difficulties posed by any use of nuclear weapons judged by the just war criteria, as I have presented them.

The single most obviously relevant fact to any moral assessment of the use of nuclear weapons is their immense power and destructiveness. This is well brought out in the 1979 survey of the effects of nuclear war undertaken by the US Congress Office of Technology Assessment.[1] A single megaton attack, with an explosive power equivalent to a million tons of TNT, on a city of the size of Detroit would cause at least 220,000 prompt fatalities and a further 420,000 casualties, many of whom would subsequently die. A US attack, involving 73 explosions varying from 40 kilotons to 170 kilotons (equivalent to 170,000 tons of TNT), which was designed to eliminate Soviet oil-refining capacity but with no attempt to minimise casualties, would cause immediate deaths ranging from some 800,000 to nearly 1½ million, the extent of casualties depending — *inter alia* — on the nature of the attack (air or surface burst) and the type of domestic accommodation assumed (single or multi-storey). A comprehensive counterforce attack against US land-based ICBM silos and facilities would cause prompt fatalities ranging from 1 million to 20 million, according to the assumptions, including the extent of prior evacuation, nature of the attack, weather conditions and time of year. 'The low end of this range (deaths below the 8 to 10 million level)', the report comments, 'requires quite optimistic assumptions, while the high end of the range is plausible only on the assumption that the attack is not preceded by a crisis period during which civilians are educated about fallout protection.'[2] An all-out attack on US urban-industrial and military targets could kill within the first 30 days between 20 million and 160 million people — that is, between 10 per cent and 77 per cent of the US population — depending on a variety of factors, including the degree of evacuation and fallout protection assumed.

Such could be the direct and immediate effects of major strategic nuclear attacks in which no effort had been made to minimise casualties. The longer-term effects would be far worse and the damage would not necessarily be confined to a limited spatio-temporal region. Radiation fallout, causing cancer, and ecological damage could spread the suffering over a wide geographical area and the resulting genetic malformations could extend it into the next generation and beyond. Recent studies have suggested that a major counterforce attack, involving more than 3,000 high-yield surface bursts at missile silos, could plunge much of the globe into a dark and arctic winter, with the sunlight obscured by clouds of dust and smoke.[3] Although the winter would be temporary, its effect on plant life and food production could persist. Catastrophic ecological effects might even be triggered by a 'smaller' attack (1,000 explosions over 100 cities with a total yield of 100 megatons) because of the amount of smoke and debris generated into the upper atmosphere by the multiple city conflagrations. Such findings are a matter of dispute among experts and are, inevitably, to an extent speculative and prone to error because of the welcome lack of experimental data. But they do serve to underline emphatically the disaster which any large-scale use of nuclear weapons would cause.

These effects all relate to the use of intercontinental strategic systems. But even any wholescale use of theatre nuclear weapons (some of which are many times the size of the Hiroshima bomb) could be very damaging if used in the densely-populated areas of central Europe. (The distinction between strategic and theatre systems is based more on the location of their possible use and range of their delivery systems than on the role or even the explosive power of the weapons.) The 1955 simulated war game, imprudently named 'Carte Blanche', suggested that the detonation of 355 theatre nuclear weapons over two days against military targets, mainly in West Germany, would leave 1½ million civilians dead and 3½ million wounded, even without the residual effects of radiation. These results helped terminate any speculation that, even if strategic weapons were unusable to secure a classical military victory, theatre nuclear weapons might provide a way of continuing conventional war by other means.

These facts are stunning and appalling. But not all uses of nuclear weapons need be as devastating. It is sometimes fashionable to talk of 'the bomb' as if it were a single homogeneous kind of weapon. There is, however, a bewildering multiplicity of types of nuclear weapons whose destructive power can range from a fraction of a kiloton, via a Hiroshima-size bomb (some 13 kilotons) up to weapons — very few now retained by the US but more still held in the Soviet inventory — of a multimegaton variety: a hundred and even a thousand times the size of the Hiroshima bomb. Moreover, the amount of damage caused would depend not just on the explosive power and radioactive yield of the weapons but many other factors. These include: the nature of the detonation (for example, air or surface burst); the precision with which the weapon is delivered (very high accuracy is now possible); and the choice of targets, particularly their proximity to population centres. Some uses of nuclear weapons might cause no civilian death — for example, their use in anti-submarine warfare or a 'demonstration' shot. Moreover, unless one assumes the inevitability of escalation, the suffering caused by the use of a low-yield theatre nuclear weapon precisely aimed at a military target even in central Europe would be of a very different order of magnitude from that caused by a major strategic nuclear exchange. There are thus important and morally significant differences between the various kinds of nuclear weapons and their possible uses, although the significance of these differences depends crucially on what is assumed about the likelihood of escalation.

Do these facts set nuclear weapons totally apart morally from conventional weapons? Certainly nuclear weapons are both more instantaneously devastating and have more insidious and persistent long-term effects than most conventional weapons, although chemical and biological weapons have their own peculiarly horrific effects. It is easier to conceive of a conventional conflict in which non-combatant casualties are minimal: the Falklands War is a good example. None the less, it is salutary to recall that the way conventional weapons have, in practice, been used in this century — at least when vital national interests were perceived to be at stake — has involved very substantial civilian casualties. Over 50 million people, the majority civilians, died in the Second World War, conventional until the very end. It is estimated that over 10 million people have been killed in conventional wars since then. Given the increasing power, sophistication and destructiveness of conventional armaments, any major conflict between the two power blocs in the heavily-populated territory of central Europe would be devastating, even if successfully confined to the conventional level.

The risk of escalation to the nuclear level would, moreover, be present from the first conventional shot. The near boundless power of nuclear weapons brings into the sharpest perspective the moral difficulties posed by the use of modern weaponry. But there is no vast and absolute moral gulf between nuclear and conventional armaments. Any major conventional conflict would be a moral tragedy.

Against this background, let us now assess the moral legitimacy of warfare involving possible use of nuclear weapons against each of the just war criteria identified in previous chapters. This assessment does not, of course, presuppose that such a failure of deterrence is at all likely: on the contrary, for the reasons adduced in Chapter 1, it is highly improbable. It is, none the less, essential to an understanding of the ethics of deterrence to appreciate the moral difficulties associated with the use of nuclear weapons.

We begin with the conditions that need to be satisfied before a state can justly resort to war, i.e. the *jus ad bellum*.

War is authorised by a competent authority.

It has been suggested that the timescale in which a decision would be required whether to respond to a nuclear attack would be so short as to preclude implementation of the full established democratic procedures for sanctioning the resort to war. But this would appear to assume that war between NATO and the Warsaw Pact might start with a surprise nuclear attack, descending as an unheralded 'bolt from the blue'. This scenario, although fashionable in the early 1950s, is very implausible. As argued in Chapter 1, since at least the early 1960s neither side has been in a position physically to disarm the other by such a pre-emptive first strike, the rationality of which is therefore deeply suspect (quite apart from the risk that the initiator of such an attack could himself be engulfed in the resulting ecological catastrophe). If the use of nuclear weapons in an East-West conflict is conceivable at all, it is more likely to arise after a period of political crisis and, probably, the inception of conventional war. If so, there would be time for the required emergency powers and other preparations for war to be duly authorised. Indeed, the agonising decision on the resort to war is more likely to be whether to respond, not to a surprise nuclear attack, but to an initially conventional attack, in the knowledge that the ensuing conflict could escalate to the nuclear level. The requirement of competent authority would thus appear to pose no special difficulty for a war between nuclear powers.

As a last resort, all available peaceful means of settling the dispute having been first tried and failed.

NATO policy, as noted in Chapter 1, is never to use weapons of any kind — conventional or nuclear — except in response to attack. Whether a state meets this requirement depends, however, not just on whether it has no alternative to the resort to force, given the impasse with which it is faced, but also the extent to which it has genuinely and strenuously sought to avoid that impasse by every available alternative, for example diplomatic, means of resolving the dispute. Subject to such caveats, there would seem no over-riding reason why this condition could not be met and, indeed, its vital importance is urgently underlined by the potential catastrophe which any war between nuclear powers could occasion.

For the sake of a just cause.

It is sometimes claimed that there can be no just cause for nuclear war. But this claim would appear somewhat muddled. In part, it may reflect the cultural and ethical relativism, criticised in Chapter 2, that would seek to drain of substance the concept of just cause. In part, it seems to conflate the requirement of just cause with the other requirements of the just war tradition. For it is a key feature of the tradition that a just cause, of itself, does not license war if, in Vitoria's words, quoted earlier, 'greater evils follow from the war itself than are averted by the war'. War is only licit if the other requirements of the just war tradition are also met. But from this it does not follow that the cause is not just but rather that not every just cause for war should be acted on. Indeed, as argued in Chapter 2, the defence of our country and democratic way of life from attack by a totalitarian aggressor, deeply hostile to political and religious freedom, would constitute a just cause by the canons of the just war, provided the attack had not been provoked by the West's own bellicose and threatening behaviour.

It has also been suggested that, as with the requirement of competent authority, the speed with which the decision would have to be taken whether or not to use nuclear weapons would allow insufficient time for consideration of the justice or otherwise of the cause. But, as already argued, such a decision is more likely to arise, if at all, only after a period of political tension and, probably, the inception of conventional conflict. Time would therefore have been available for the necessary moral assessment, provided it had been so used. But this suggestion does stress how incumbent upon our political leaders it would be to have given deep and serious moral thought to the agonising moral choice with which they might be faced long before crisis point was reached, when time could, indeed, be short.

The harm judged likely to result from war is not disproportionate to the likely good aimed at (as specified by the just cause) taking into account the probability of success.

It is with this first application of the requirement of proportionality that the particular difficulties posed for nuclear weapons begins.

We have — mercifully — been spared any major conflict between nuclear powers. The experience which we would therefore bring to undertake this assessment would be meagre, while any errors in our judgement could be, literally, catastrophic. As stressed in Chapter 2, the god-like calculation required to assess the likely balance of good and ill that would result from a major conventional war is a daunting task. The difficulties would be immeasurably magnified if the conflict involved nuclear powers and hence risked the use of nuclear weapons.

In assessing whether resistance, either at the conventional or nuclear level, to aggression by a nuclear power would meet the requirement of proportionality it would be necessary to weigh in the balance, on the one hand, the magnitude and probability of the evil that would thereby be averted, as specified by the just cause, and on the other, of the suffering that could result from resistance. Much would therefore depend on the assessment made of the degree and likelihood of escalation. Resistance could clearly not be justified if it would inevitably lead to a massive strategic nuclear exchange since the resulting devastation would be such that no conceivable good could outweigh and no sane person count as success. However great the justice of the cause, this can hardly license such destruction that the cause itself ceases to exist whether through the literal obliteration of the state being defended or the commission of mass murder on such a genocidal scale as to undermine the value of the way of life being defended, including our collective abhorrence of genocide.

But the conclusion that resistance could never in any circumstances be justified against a nuclear aggressor would itself be inimical to the just war tradition, in view of its recognition that resistance to wicked aggression may be not merely permissible but also a moral duty. Resistance could be licit if the probability were high that it would lead the aggressor to desist from his attack well before disproportionate levels of suffering were reached. But, given all the uncertainties and risks involved, it would — even if not impossible — clearly be very difficult for the requirement of proportion to be satisfied: a conclusion which would apply even if the resistance contemplated were at the conventional level, still more the nuclear level.

We turn next to the conditions that need to be satisfied if a war can be waged justly, i.e. the *jus in bello*.

Harm likely to result from a particular military operation should not be disproportionate to the good aimed at.

In Chapter 2 we distinguished between the various levels at which the principle of proportion should be applied to the conduct of war: in particular, the politico-military level at which decisions are taken about the application of military force to achieve the ends of policy, where the harm that may result has to be assessed, ultimately, against the justice or otherwise of the war's cause; and the lesser tactical decisions taken by military commanders in the field. Since the only use of nuclear weapons recognised by NATO would be to achieve a political objective (to persuade the aggressor to desist from his aggression) and be subject to political control, this distinction would appear to be irrelevant to nuclear weapons. Any use of nuclear weapons — however small — would be a crucial political decision. Nuclear weapons are too important for their use to be delegated to commanders in the field.

The moral constraints presented by the application of the principle of proportion to a decision whether to resort to war in the nuclear era would thus press hard on any contemplated use of nuclear weapons in the conduct of the war. The limited use of nuclear weapons might be deemed a proportionate use of force — depending on the scale and imminence of the evil that would thereby be averted and the probability of escalation. But any wholesale use of nuclear weapons would be ruled out because the suffering thereby caused would be disproportionate.

Non-combatant casualties should be minimised as far as possible.

In Chapter 3 I argued that military action involving risk to non-combatants may be morally licit where the risk is judged small or where efforts have been made to minimise it, but there is a very strong moral presumption against military action that it is known would inevitably cause non-combatant deaths, even where these are unintended. The inhabitants of Moscow or Washington could reasonably regard the distinction as somewhat metaphysical that they had been incinerated as the result of a multimegaton attack on military targets within the city rather than as the result of a deliberate counter-population attack.

Some specialised uses of nuclear weapons — for example, as noted earlier, in anti-submarine warfare — might cause no non-combatant casualty and could, hence, meet this requirement. But quite apart from the risk of escalation, there is an immense moral presumption against most uses of nuclear weapons because, even where civilian targets are deliberately avoided, non-combatants could still be at risk from radiation fallout. None the less, I have argued that military action causing certain non-combatant deaths may still be morally permissible — despite the enormous presumption against this — if there is very good reason to believe that this is the *only* way to prevent a very great harm and that the good thereby achieved would clearly and decisively outweigh the harm: where non-combatants are involved, a mere balance of probable good over ill is not enough. Our discussion of area bombing in the Second World War has already illustrated the very considerable difficulties in meeting both these conditions even in conventional warfare and the difficulties would be immensely compounded if nuclear weapons might be used.

It might, however, be possible to justify against these conditions the limited use of nuclear weapons against military targets, even where non-combatant casualties were bound to result, provided efforts had been made to reduce these, as evidenced by the choice of target, precision of aim, mode of attack and size and yield of weapon used. But deliberate attacks against cities would appear to be forbidden, both because it is difficult to conceive what good could clearly and decisively outweigh the massive non-combatant suffering thereby caused and because it could hardly be claimed that such counter-population attacks were the only possible response to aggression, given the plethora of military targets, their greater relevance to the conflict and the availability of means to attack them with reasonable precision (a capability conspicuously lacking, particularly in the early years of the Second World War). Moreover, any very large-scale use of nuclear weapons even against military targets, such as a comprehensive counterforce attack, would be precluded because of the immense collateral damage caused to non-combatants. Finally, whether any use of nuclear weapons — however restrained — could be deemed discriminate would depend crucially on the assumed likelihood of escalation.

This initial application of the just war theory to possible uses of nuclear weapons suggests that, although many of the criteria do not pose special difficulties for nuclear weapons, those of proportion (as applied both to the resort to war and to its conduct) and of noncombatant immunity do. Even a major conventional conflict would risk breaching these principles. But the devastating power of nuclear weapons makes the moral difficulties associated with their use particularly acute. Any wholesale use of strategic nuclear weapons even against military targets, still more cities, would be morally impermissible. No moral casuistry can sanction the inception of Armageddon. More limited uses against military targets might be morally licit but whether or not this is so would depend critically on the prospects of escalation. We shall therefore need to address further the problem of escalation. But in view of the strong moral presumption already apparent against any use of nuclear weapons, it is clearly necessary to consider whether a coherent and effective defence policy could be formulated which did not rely on nuclear weapons.

5 ALTERNATIVES TO DETERRENCE

According to the just war tradition, there is a moral presumption against war and, as the arguments of the last chapter have shown, a very strong moral presumption against any use of nuclear weapons. In view of this, there is obvious attraction in a policy that simply refuses to have anything to do with nuclear weapons, regardless of what else happens. But, as I have sought to argue, it is not enough to proclaim that justice should be done, though the heavens fall, particularly when, as in the nuclear era, the all too literal collapse of the heavens may be at stake. We have also to have regard to the consequences of our actions and the complexities of the human predicament in which the use of force may sometimes be necessary to constrain the ambitions of wicked men, lest the innocent suffer. For this reason, the just war tradition, while proclaiming the presumption against war, also recognises that it may be not merely morally permissible but even a moral duty for a nation to defend its own people and way of life against unjust aggression.

Applying these principles to the situation with which the West is faced, we need to fashion a policy which will help to prevent war and, in particular, any use of nuclear weapons, while also securing our political liberties and way of life. NATO's policy of deterrence, as argued in Chapter 1, attempts to meet both these objectives. But such deterrence appears ultimately based on an intention to use nuclear weapons, the implementation of which would be beset with grave moral difficulties. What is required, therefore, is to consider whether there is any alternative security system available to NATO which could meet these twin objectives, while avoiding such moral difficulties. I shall consider five possible options.

Each option is designed to eliminate the nuclear component in NATO's deterrent policy. Many critics of NATO policy have, of course, not wished to go as far as this or, at least, not forthwith. And clearly many intermediate positions are possible between NATO's present deterrent policy and a complete non-nuclear policy for the Alliance. These might include, for example, some or all of the following measures:[1] unilateral renunciation by the United Kingdom and France of their nuclear weapons, leaving the United States as the sole repository of nuclear force in the West; the establishment of a nuclear-weapon-free zone in Europe 'from Poland to Portugal' requiring, on the West's part, not merely the non-nuclear status of France and the United Kingdom but also the unilateral withdrawal of all US nuclear weapons from the soil of Europe or adjacent waters; deep cuts in the superpowers' nuclear arsenals; the adoption by NATO of a policy never to be the first to use nuclear weapons.

Some of these positions, and the merits of a no-first-use policy in particular, will be explored further in Chapter 8. But to meet the ethical dilemma we are currently addressing such measures would only be relevant in so far as they constituted the first steps towards the achievement by NATO of a complete non-nuclear policy. For if any form of nuclear deterrence is morally impermissible, insuperable moral difficulties would still beset NATO's defence policy even if the nuclear component were much reduced, removed from European soil and entrusted to only one member of the Alliance. Morality would rather require that the West should not merely modify but withdraw from such an ethically untenable position, perhaps not at once but at least within some definite and not unduly protracted timescale. The aim of the present chapter is therefore to explore not modifications but alternatives to nuclear deterrence.

The first option to be considered is that of unilateral complete pacifism in international relations. Under this policy, the West would give up not merely its nuclear weapons but its conventional ones as well, apart from those required for purely internal security purposes which, in the UK's case, would include a capability to counter the IRA threat. These steps would be taken even in the absence of any readiness on the part of the Warsaw Pact to follow suit. The West would thus signal that it was neither willing nor able to offer any resistance to an external aggressor.

The merits of this policy are twofold. First, it would ensure that we did not engage in morally impermissible wrongdoing in the defence of our country, whether through the use of nuclear or conventional weapons, the use of either of which — as argued in the last chapter — could present moral difficulties. Secondly, a pacifist policy would help to prevent war and the use of nuclear weapons. It would not, of course, remove the risk that we could still be incinerated as innocent bystanders in a conflict between other nuclear powers. But a policy of complete and absolute readiness to surrender would at least remove any reason for an adversary to use conventional or nuclear weapons against us. These then are the advantages of unilateral complete pacifism. But the disadvantages are massive. To be effective, our readiness to surrender must be total. For if there is any demand imposed on us that we are not prepared to concede, an adversary could threaten the use of force and, if that failed, use force — if necessary, nuclear force — to secure compliance. A nation following this path would thus be obliged to concede any demand of his adversary, however wicked and unscrupulous that enemy might be, and however wicked and evil might be his demands. No doubt we would hope that such demands would not be made. But the policy is presumably not a temporary aberration and may well have to last a long time. Unfortunately, history offers little realistic ground for believing that a rival nation would not — sooner or later — seek to exploit our self-imposed weakness nor that such exploitation might not be morally and politically very difficult to accept. Had such a policy been pursued, we would, for example, have been powerless to prevent the Nazi domination of the world and the full implementation of Hitler's genocidal plans.

Whether any nation would be able, in practice, consistently to follow such a policy of self-abnegation and impotence, given human nature as it is, seems deeply doubtful, as does the moral propriety of such a policy. It is one thing to concede, as I have in the last two chapters, that some acts of force may have such appalling consequences as to render them morally impermissible. It is quite another to argue that any use of force would be morally precluded simply because it would occasion some moral harm. For in the post-lapsarian world we inhabit it may sometimes be necessary to do an act which involves moral harm if this is the only way to prevent much greater harm being done to others. To suppose otherwise is to presuppose the absolute moral distinction between acts and omissions which I have argued is untenable. It is to assume that our moral integrity can be preserved by inactivity even when that inactivity causes immense suffering to others: whether those for whom we have a particular responsibility, such as that which a government has towards the people with whose care and defence it has been entrusted, or those for whom we may have a more general moral responsibility, such as the Jews under threat of Hitler's final solution. Indeed, had Hitler been allowed to fulfil his genocidal plans unimpeded, our inactivity could have been described as other than gross wrongdoing only by the most specious play on words: for such non-intervention would assuredly have been the wrong thing to do. It is, therefore, hardly surprising that such a pacifist position is quite inconsistent with the just war tradition.

The next option to be considered is that of unilateral nuclear pacifism. Even if the Soviet Union were unwilling — as it has made abundantly clear that it is — to abandon its nuclear weapons, NATO would abolish its own nuclear arsenal, at the same time, perhaps, increasing its conventional capability to a level at which it could offer a more robust and prolonged defence against conventional attack. We would thus signal our willingness and ability to resist conventional aggression but not nuclear.

The attraction of such a policy is that it might appear to offer a way of securing some of the advantages of complete pacifism — the forswearing of the ethically dubious use of nuclear weapons by ourselves, and the reduction in the risk that others would use them against us — while avoiding the more extreme disadvantages of complete pacifism. For we would still retain the capability to deal with aggression by a non-nuclear power and would be able to offer at least some resistance to a nuclear power.

But would unilateral nuclear pacifism achieve these objectives? As argued in Chapter 1, the nuclear superpowers are mutually deterred from using military force against each other, provided:

(i) Each side has the ability, if attacked by the other, to inflict on the attacker sufficient harm to outweigh any conceivable gain to be secured from the attack.
(ii) Neither side can rule out that the other might use this ability, if attacked.

The first condition would no longer be met if the West were unilaterally to disarm. The use of military force, including nuclear force, would therefore once again become a rational option for the remaining nuclear superpower to exploit against the other superpower or his allies, for the costs of such action would no longer necessarily appear prohibitively high. Even if we chose to resist any aggression only by conventional means, a determined nuclear power could decide to put an end to such resistance by initially threatening and, if that failed, by using nuclear weapons: an escalatory move to which we would be powerless to respond and, in view of our impotence in the face of which, our decision to resort to war would appear of doubtful moral legitimacy given the inadequate prospect of success. And the irony is that the more effective our conventional defence, the greater would be a nuclear aggressor's incentive to use his nuclear weapons to overcome opposition to the achievement of his plans. The conventional forces so expensively built up would thus be useless at least against a determined nuclear power.

Moreover, an adversary enjoying such a nuclear monopoly could exploit the threat and, if necessary, the use of nuclear weapons to overcome opposition not merely to plans for territorial conquest but also the many more subtle ways of promoting his political influence in order to align the West's foreign and domestic policies to suit his interests. We would thus be open to all forms of nuclear coercion but this massive disadvantage would not have been offset by any lessening of the risk of war and of nuclear attack: indeed, quite the reverse, since the conditions for stable mutual deterrence would no longer obtain. As the first option has shown, the only way entirely to remove such risk would be a policy of complete and absolute readiness to surrender to an adversary's demands, however wicked and evil. But if we were to adopt such a policy of surrender, our position would then collapse into and be open to all the objections — moral and political — of the first option.

Unilateral nuclear pacifism is thus faced with the following cruel dilemma. The more it seeks to achieve the first objective of preventing war and the use of nuclear weapons, the more it is pushed towards a policy of complete surrender and impotence, inconsistent with the just war tradition. But the more it seeks to achieve the second objective of securing our political liberty and preventing wrongful aggression, the more it increases the risk of war and hence the risk that nuclear weapons will be used, given that the conditions for stable mutual deterrence no longer hold. Nor does conventional defence offer an escape from this dilemma, since there can be no effective conventional defence against a determined nuclear aggressor.

Unilateral nuclear pacifism might still appear to offer a way of ensuring that — whatever else happens — we at least are not guilty of the use of nuclear weapons. This might represent a decisive moral gain if deterrence necessarily depended upon morally impermissible uses of nuclear weapons. But, although we have conceded that there is a strong moral presumption against use of nuclear weapons, it has yet to be established that any use would be morally impermissible. We have, moreover, yet to consider the precise relation between deterrence and use. But unless such a very strong claim can be established, any balanced ethical evaluation must also address what else would happen as the result of the adoption of unilateral nuclear pacifism: in particular the increased risk that innocents would suffer from a major conventional war and the use of nuclear weapons by the remaining nuclear super-power — a risk that, as we have seen, could only be removed by a policy of total surrender, indistinguishable from that required by complete pacifism and vulnerable to the same moral objections.

Moreover, precisely because of these inherent difficulties in the nuclear pacifist stance, it may be questionable whether it would be able to meet the legitimate requirement of any government defence policy that it should be able to survive in bad times as well as good. Rather, it seems that unilateral nuclear pacifism might be no more durable in a crisis than the pacifism in the 1920s and 1930s which, having encouraged governments to allow Nazi power to expand unchecked, was finally abandoned in the face of Nazi aggression. There would thus appear some risk that a policy of unilateral nuclear pacifism, adopted in a period of beguiling international calm, would not survive the pressures of the imminent or actual conflict to whose occurrence it might have contributed by under-mining the conditions for stable mutual deterrence. It seems, indeed, rather more likely that, given human nature as it is, the policy would be reversed and our political leaders would seek to reapply the nuclear knowledge rather than concede such an over-whelming one-sided advantage to an adversary. But such reapplica-tion might come too late to restore peace based on deterrence and, under the escalatory pressures of conventional warfare, could lead to use. Thus unilateral nuclear pacifism — however unintentionally — could lead to the very nuclear war it had been designed to avert.

The third option I wish to explore is a policy of unilateral nuclear pacifism allied to a system of strategic defence. As in the previous option, the West would unilaterally dismantle its own nuclear weapons but would be protected by a network of defensive systems designed to counter any Soviet missile threat. The attraction of this option is that the combination of nuclear pacifism and strategic defence might appear a way of avoiding the objections to which either policy on its own is vulnerable. The objections to unilateral nuclear pacifism have just been enumerated. The principal objec-tion to strategic defence, while nuclear weapons are retained, is that — as argued in Chapter 1 — it would, if achievable, threaten to upset the conditions for stable mutual deterrence by appearing to offer a way of neutralising the other side's retaliatory capability. It might thus make the use of nuclear weapons appear a possible rational option. This objection would no longer apply if the weapons had been given up. Indeed, President Reagan seemed to be appealing to this line of argument in his March 1983 address exploring the concept of strategic defence. In that address he called on 'the scientific community who gave us nuclear weapons to turn their great talents to the cause of mankind and world peace, to give us the means of rendering these nuclear weapons impotent and obsolete'.[2]

This is a deeply enticing prospect. Unfortunately, both its feasibility and its coherence are suspect. There could be difficulty constructing such a network without some use of nuclear warheads for its anti-missile missiles. More importantly, if the adoption by NATO of unilateral nuclear pacifism is to escape the objections levelled against it, such a defensive screen would need to provide a permanent 100 per cent guarantee against nuclear attack, embracing the whole of NATO territory. For anything less than such a permanent guarantee — given the immense destructiveness of nuclear weapons — would not be enough, while a screen protecting the US homeland but not Europe would not only leave Europe vulnerable but expose the US to nuclear coercion from threats to its allies. As argued in Chapter 1, however, it is extremely doubtful that such a permanent guarantee against ballistic missile attack could be provided, while a substantial threat would still remain from non-ballistic missile systems. But if, to guard against such threats, some nuclear weapons were retained as a supplement to the strategic defence system, we would merely have risked weakening the conditions of stable mutual deterrence without having achieved any genuine alternative to deterrence. The vain quest for the perfect defensive screen would have been costly and unsettling to arms control.

The fourth option is that of multilateral nuclear pacifism but without any other significant change in present political structures and relations. Under this scenario, all the present nuclear powers would abandon their nuclear weapons but otherwise the deep antagonisms between the rival political systems would remain unchanged. This is obviously not an option realisable in the immediate future. Indeed, as described, it is an implausible option:

it is certainly very difficult to believe that the nuclear powers would consent to a complete disbandment of their nuclear arsenals in the absence of massively improved political relations. Despite its implausibility, the option is none the less worthy of consideration.

Would such a nuclear disarmed world be safer? It may seem self-evident that it would, but this is questionable. So long as men remain prone to wickedness — to greed, selfishness and all the other vices to which the fallen human condition is subject — so will the causes of conflict abound. The merit of nuclear weapons is that they remove the incentive to initiate such conflicts by rendering their cost prohibitively high. But, without nuclear weapons and in the absence of radical changes in the global political structures or the underlying human nature that they express, such a policy could merely encourage a regression to the habit of regular conventional warfare that has so scarred the history of Europe by making it appear that the world was once again safe for major conventional war. But such wars, as noted earlier, have been deeply devastating events and would now be even more so, given the massive increase in the sophistication and destructiveness of conventional weaponry since the Second World War. Moreover, as with the option of unilateral nuclear pacifism, the risk would still remain that under the stress of imminent or actual war, the nuclear knowledge — which can never be erased from human consciousness — would be reapplied. It is surely difficult to see either a Hitler or a Churchill succumbing to conventional defeat if this could be avoided by resurrecting the nuclear option. It was, of course, precisely the fear that the other side would acquire nuclear weapons that fuelled the search for them during the Second World War. The only difference this time would be that it would not take five years to achieve the nuclear breakthrough. Thus, despite the common assumption that the mere physical removal of nuclear weapons would be a decisive moral gain, this is at least open to question. It could merely render major conventional — and hence nuclear — war more likely.

Is there then no hope of a world freed from the tyranny of nuclear weapons? This possibility will be explored by my fifth and final option. Under this scenario there has been a radical and total transformation of the world political structure. No longer do two suspicious power blocs glare menacingly at each other, surrounded by a host of lesser nation-states oscillating in and out of the power blocs' spheres of influence, while regarding their own regional neighbours with mutual suspicion. Rather, all nations of the world are united together in a common confederation of states whose external relations are presided over by a benign and democratically-constituted world authority, which alone possesses the military power to enforce sanctions against any nation threatening the international equilibrium. Nuclear weapons have long been banned from national armouries and the world authority carries out regular and reliable inspections to ensure that the ban remains fully in force. In such a world the risk of nuclear war, if not entirely eliminated, might be considered very small.

In present circumstances this is a deeply utopian vision, although — as I shall explore in the final chapter — perhaps not necessarily for ever unattainable. As a long-term goal, this vision — not every detail of which may necessarily be essential — seems eminently worth striving for. Moreover, some steps, however small and tentative, towards its attainment may even now be within our power. But its full achievement, if feasible at all, is clearly a very distant prospect. To pretend otherwise — to act now as if we were in or about to enter such a utopia — would be irresponsible. It would also be disingenuous to use the imminence of such a utopia as grounds for minimising any ethical difficulties associated with nuclear deterrence.

Our survey of the possible alternatives to deterrence suggests that multilateral nuclear pacifism, accompanied by a radical transformation in global political relationships, could provide a way of meeting the objectives of preventing war, while securing our political liberties, but is not a choice at present realistically available. A technological solution, such as that offered by comprehensive strategic defence, is unlikely to be forthcoming. The only alternatives to nuclear deterrence currently available would therefore appear to be unilateral pacifism, whether complete or nuclear, and to either of these options there are grave objections.

It might none the less be suggested that a unilateral pacifist option is still preferable to nuclear deterrence. Our choice between the options has to be made in conditions of uncertainty, where we cannot be sure precisely what probability to assign to the various outcomes of our choice or even precisely how these outcomes should be evaluated. In such conditions of uncertainty, it might be argued that the rational principle of choice to apply would be the 'maximin' principle: i.e. to choose that policy whose worst possible outcome is less bad than the worst possible outcome of any alternative policy. On such grounds it might appear rational to opt for unilateral complete pacifism on the grounds that its worst possible outcome — political subjugation and international impotence — would be preferable to either conventional war and nuclear attack, followed by political subjugation, the worst outcome of unilateral nuclear pacifism, or conventional and nuclear war, the worst possible outcome of a failure of deterrence. Moreover, even if complete pacifism is ruled out because of its doubtful practicality and high moral and political cost, this ranking of outcomes might still suggest that unilateral nuclear pacifism would be preferable to nuclear deterrence.

But this argument does not work. First, the worst possible outcome of the adoption in peacetime of unilateral nuclear pacifism could be even worse than that assumed. For we have suggested earlier grounds for doubting whether such a policy would be able to survive the pressures of a conventional conflict whose occurrence it would have rendered more likely and hence whether it might not, however unintentionally, lead to nuclear war. If so, the worst possible outcome of the peacetime adoption of nuclear pacifism would be the same as that of the failure of deterrence: the only difference being the increased probability of that outcome being brought about by nuclear pacifism.

It is, in any case, very doubtful whether the maximin principle, even if — as some would doubt — it is valid, is applicable to the present choice. For there are at least two crucial respects in which it differs from the simplified scenarios to which some philosophers have suggested it might have application.[3] First, the uncertainty under which we have to decide is by no means complete. In particular, there is good reason, as I have tried to show, to assign a very low probability to the failure of deterrence but a very high probability, if not certainty, that sooner or later the self-imposed weakness demanded by either of the pacifist options would be exploited by an adversary. Secondly, application of the maximin principle is designed to ensure an outcome that, if not the best available, is at least acceptable. But neither our own political subjugation and impotence to prevent unjust aggression against others — the worst outcome of unilateral complete pacifism — nor conventional war, partial nuclear incineration, followed by political subjugation, even accepting this as the worst possible outcome of unilateral nuclear pacifism, can be deemed remotely acceptable outcomes, morally or politically. It would thus appear of very dubious rationality to opt for a policy that would significantly increase the risk that such unacceptable outcomes would occur.

It is therefore implausible to suppose that maximin or, indeed, any other simplifying decision-making procedure is appropriate to the present complex and agonising choice. We need rather to consider which, if any, of the currently available policy options is most likely to secure the twin objectives of preventing war and, in particular, the use of nuclear weapons, and at the same time securing our political liberties and way of life. Unilateral complete pacifism may achieve the former objective, but not the latter. Unilateral nuclear pacifism, in so far as it does not collapse into complete pacifism, risks the loss of our political liberty, without removing — indeed increasing — the risk of conventional war and nuclear attack. In present circumstances, only nuclear deterrence appears to offer a good prospect of securing both objectives, of helping to preserve peace and freedom. It thus appears the rational option to prefer.

But if nuclear deterrence appears the only way at present of meeting both the objectives we have derived from the just war tradition, it also appears challenged by that tradition because of the moral objections to the use of nuclear weapons. The prescriptions of the just war tradition appear thus to point in divergent directions. A possible escape from this impasse would be if deterrence could be divorced from use in such a way that we could enjoy the beneficial effects of deterrence, without facing the moral difficulties of use. It might then be possible for nuclear deterrence to be morally justified, even if any use of the weapons were regarded as morally impermissible. I shall consider in the next chapter whether this is a coherent position.

6 DETERRENCE AND INTENTIONS

It is often claimed that intentions are crucial to deterrence and hence to its moral evaluation. I propose, therefore, to consider first what intentions, if any, are required to underlie deterrence and then to provide a moral evaluation of the intentions. My concern is not primarily to give a factual description of the intentions which are held by those at present involved in the deterrence business but rather to give an analysis of what intentions are logically required to underline deterrence if it is to have the features normally attributed to it by its advocates.

Before addressing this question it will be helpful to consider some of the logical features of the concept of intention itself that have been identified by philosophers. Not surprisingly, here, as elsewhere in philosophy, there is no unanimous view of the correct philosophical analysis of the concept. But it is generally agreed that the following features are important.

First, there is a distinction between an expression of intention, acting with an intention and acting intentionally.[1] Some of the intentions we express are 'pure' intentions — that is, like Davidson's example of the man who intends to build a squirrel house but never gets round to doing so, they do not necessarily lead to action.[2] In the case of acting with an intention, the action itself may be intentional, e.g. firing a gun, as well as being undertaken with an intention, e.g. to shoot a man.

Secondly, if I intend to do X then I must in some sense regard doing X as desirable and also possible. Davidson, for example, says, 'To intend to perform an action is to hold that it is desirable to perform an action of a certain sort in the light of what one believes is or will be the case.'[3] As regards possibility, Stuart Hampshire says, 'To intend something to happen (as the result of my activity) is at least to believe that it may or could happen.'[4]

The final feature of the concept of intention worth noticing at this stage is that how we characterise an intention depends, in part, on how many of the consequences of the intended act we choose to include in the description. This so-called 'accordion effect'[5] is illustrated by Anscombe's well-known example:

71

A man is pumping water into the cistern which supplies the drinking water of a house. Someone has found a way of systematically contaminating the source with a deadly cumulative poison whose effects are unnoticeable until they can no longer be cured. The house is regularly inhabited by a small group of party chiefs, with their immediate families, who are in control of a great state; they are engaged in exterminating the Jews . . .

What intention does the man have in moving his arm up and down? It would be correct to say: to pump water into the house, to replenish the water supply, to poison the inhabitants. Could we also say that he is saving the Jews? Anscombe thinks not, on the grounds that 'this further description e.g. to save the Jews . . . is not such that we can now say: he is saving the Jews'.[6]

As Anscombe has described the example this is perhaps true, since that particular consequence is rather remote and loosely connected with the action as described. But if we tighten up the example and add further background details, some such intention may be correctly attributable. For example, let us suppose that the water pumper had discovered that the house is occupied by Nazi chiefs who are putting the finishing touches to a plan to exterminate the Jews, the details of which they and only they know and which will be implemented as soon as their deliberations are complete. In that case the man could legitimately be held to have the intention to prevent a Nazi plot to exterminate the Jews. But once the consequences become too remote and ill-connected with the action, their use to characterise the intention underlying the action becomes implausible. Thus Caesar's assassins could hardly legitimately characterise their intention as being 'to stop a bung hole' on the grounds that:

Imperious Caesar dead and turn'd to clay
Might stop a hole to keep the wind away.
(Hamlet Act V Sc. 1)[7]

So much by way of preliminary philosophical analysis. Let us now consider what sort of intentions underlie nuclear deterrence.

Two alternative formulations might be suggested. First, the intention has been characterised, using the terminology just introduced, as the expression of an intention of the conditional form 'if A, X':[8] indeed, it could also be characterised as a 'pure' intention since it does not necessarily lead to the doing of X. For example: NATO will use nuclear weapons if other means have failed to prevent a Soviet attack against the Alliance. Secondly, the intention might be characterised as of the form doing Y with an intention: for example, NATO maintains a nuclear and conventional capability with the intention of thereby dissuading the Soviet Union from an attack upon the Alliance.

Let us consider the second formulation first. A number of objections have been made against this kind of formulation. First, it has been objected that a consequence such as avoiding war or preventing aggression is too remote (compare Caesar and the 'bung hole') and/or is not something that NATO could reasonably believe 'may or could happen' as a result of the action. As Paskins has argued: it 'is a further good beyond my unaided power'.[9]

This objection certainly has force against too general a description of the intention such as avoiding war, the achievement of which may well depend on too many other things besides maintaining conventional and nuclear forces. This would be comparable with 'saving the Jews' as the characterisation of the intention of Anscombe's water-pumper. But as our discussion of that example showed, the more limited aim of 'preventing a Nazi plot to exterminate the Jews' may well be a plausible characterisation of the intention. And this, it might be argued, is the case with the intention (dissuading the Soviet Union from an attack upon the Alliance) as I have characterised it. It does, of course, require another party to be dissuaded, if my intention to dissuade is to be successfully accomplished. But that is equally so with persuasion. The chairman of a company could, however, legitimately be said to be addressing a board meeting with the intention of persuading the board members to vote for a particular motion, even though, for this intention to be fulfilled, those present would have to be persuaded. The consequence — the Soviet Union being dissuaded — may thus be neither too remote nor such that NATO could not believe it 'may or could happen' as the result of its action. It could therefore be correctly included within the characterisation of the intention.

At this point it may be objected that since deterrence is an unsound doctrine, nuclear weapons will not have the dissuasive effect alleged and hence the effect is too remote from the action to be classified as the object of an intention. Indeed, I suspect that much of the motivation of those seeking to deny that NATO could have such an intention stems precisely from their belief in the doubtful effectiveness of deterrence. But this claim — even if it were well based, and the arguments of Chapter 1 suggest otherwise — is hardly decisive to the present issue. For I am simply seeking a correct description of the intention underlying this aspect of NATO strategy. NATO's political leaders — to whom this intention is most plausibly attributed — certainly believe it has this effect and, even if their belief were mistaken, this would not of itself necessitate a change in the characterisation of the intention. Just so, in Davidson's example, a man who boards a plane headed for London, Ontario in the mistaken belief that it is going to London, England still has the intention, in boarding the plane, of going to London, England.[10]

A more telling objection to this characterisation of the intention is that it does not tell us enough about how NATO expects to fulfil the dissuasion, both to enable us to decide whether it is correctly classified as an intention and, still more, to enable us to evaluate its moral status. As Paskins and Dockrill point out, we need to be able to 'differentiate the NATO method of promoting world peace from other (e.g. utopian) methods'.[11] Just as in the water-pumping example, in order to be able to assess whether it is correct to characterise the intention as preventing a Nazi plot to exterminate the Jews and to evaluate the moral quality of that intention, it is clearly relevant to know that it is to be fulfilled by poisoning the Nazi leaders.

How then does NATO expect to fulfil its intention of dissuading the Soviet Union from attack? The definition of deterrence offered in Chapter 1 was that it meant dissuading an adversary from initiating or continuing military action by posing for him the prospect that the costs of such action would exceed the gains. It may therefore be suggested that for that prospect to be successfully posed our political leaders must have the conditional intention noted in our first formulation, i.e. to use nuclear weapons if other means fail to prevent a Soviet attack upon the Alliance. But is this conditional intention strictly required? Surely the West could reasonably expect to fulfil its primary dissuasive intention without necessarily intending the use of nuclear weapons but simply through maintaining nuclear and conventional forces, relying on what McGeorge Bundy has called 'the existential deterrence'[12] of a nuclear capability.

At the extreme, this position would be that of bluff. Our political leaders — despite their public protestations to the contrary — intend never to use nuclear weapons in any circumstances but maintain a nuclear capability so that the Soviet Union will think the opposite — or at least be sufficiently uncertain so that deterrence can still work.

But the bluff hypothesis is based on a mistaken view of what is involved in maintaining a nuclear capability. For this is not a matter of simply possessing the relevant black boxes (like keeping a revolver locked in the drawer). Rather, maintaining a deterrent capability involves a whole complex set of actions and activities by a wide variety of people: scientists researching and developing the weapons (to keep the systems up to date), workers in factories making the weapons, civil servants purchasing the components, servicemen who are recruited and trained to deploy and maintain the systems in readiness for operational use and, of course, the political leaders upon whose decisions the whole system relies. Moreover, in a democracy the electorate who vote for the defence policies advocated by the political leaders are a final crucial ingredient. For deterrence to be based on bluff, our political leaders would need to deceive not just a potential adversary but all of their own people involved in the process — most crucially, the servicemen operating the system. Quite apart from the possible moral dubiety of such wholesale deception, there is the sheer impracticality of maintaining such a secret for any sustained length of time in a democracy, particularly in view of the regular changes of government. But if the secret comes out, the deterrent value of the weapons will, at best, be dangerously diminished and, at worst, lost altogether, while the morale and motivation of those involved in operating the deterrent will inevitably be undermined.

Some of the deceitfulness of this position, although certainly not the adverse effect on service morale and motivation, could perhaps be mitigated if it were accompanied by sincere public avowals of the intention never to use the weapons. It would then be necessary to rely upon the cynicism of the Soviet Union to ensure that they would discount such statements, if the deterrent value of the weapons is not to be lost. It has, indeed, been claimed that such byzantine reasoning underlies the conclusions on deterrence of the US Catholic bishops in their Pastoral Letter on War and Peace.[13] The West's position, if such a posture were adopted, would be one of double bluff. We would say that we never intend to use the weapons, intending never to use them but intending that the Soviet

Union should believe that we might. Just so, the poker player, who wishes to influence the betting of others who play before him, might say that he intends not to bet high on his hand, intending not to do so but intending that the other players should believe he will. But such double bluffs do not escape — indeed, appear even more vulnerable to — the fundamental objection to any bluffs: that they can be undermined either by failure consistently to maintain the deception or by being called. In the present case it would seem a particularly unsafe assumption upon which to rest the security of the West for all the, perhaps lengthy, time that deterrence may be required that the Soviet Union would continue always and in all circumstances to disbelieve the West's, presumably oft-repeated, sincere avowals of non-use.

Bluff — whether single or double — is thus too fragile a basis on which to rest deterrence. None the less, this discussion has still highlighted that what is essential to deterrence is not what we think so much as what the adversary thinks. Pure bluff may be impractical, but from this it does not follow that our political leaders necessarily need to have formed a firm conditional intention to use nuclear weapons. Indeed, the second requirement, specified in Chapter 1, for stable mutual deterrence was merely that neither side could rule out that the other might use his nuclear capability if attacked: not that either has firmly to believe this will happen. Thus for deterrence to remain credible and practical, what is needed is that our political leaders should not have ruled out the option of use altogether. This suggests that the minimum secondary intention logically required for deterrence to work, i.e. to fulfil the primary intention of dissuading an adversary from attack, may be of a rather more complex form than the simple conditional 'if, A, X' earlier considered. For example:

Our political leaders intend$_1$ that the Soviet Union should believe that NATO might intend$_2$ to do X, if A.

This is not bluff since our political leaders may not have ruled out possible use but equally they do not need to have decided now, in advance of knowing the precise circumstances, whether they would use them, if A were fulfilled: they thus neither intend nor do not intend to use them. They could reasonably expect to fulfil their intention to induce such uncertainty in the minds of the Soviet leadership by maintaining a nuclear capability in operational readiness coupled, if necessary, with statements of their readiness to use it. Quite how necessary such statements are is, however, a matter for debate. Certainly constantly uttered threats are neither required nor desirable. Paskins has objected to this kind of formulation of the intention. He says:

> In public our leaders insist on their resolve to use nuclear weapons if necessary . . . In secret, I presume, newcomers to high office are briefed about the careful thought that has been given to the circumstances in which it will be 'necessary' to use nuclear weapons . . . Taken together, the public pronouncements which are there for all to see and the secret positions which must exist amount to a conditional intention.[14]

But do they? On the interpretation I have offered of the secondary intention underlying deterrence, the public pronouncements (uttered to keep the other side guessing but not backed by a firm intention) certainly do not constitute proof of intention. What then of the secret contingency planning? No doubt Paskins is right to assume this exists — indeed it is an absolute requirement of maintaining the deterrent in a state of operational readiness. Moreover, as I shall argue later, the kind of plans maintained are relevant to the moral assessment of deterrence. But the existence of contingency plans does not constitute an intention to implement them. Contingency plans rather provide options for possible use and, indeed, options which may be incapable of all being fulfilled at the same time. There is a world of difference between having a contingency plan, even exercising that plan, and actually taking a decision in the real world to implement it.

But if the secondary intention, whereby NATO expects to dissuade the Soviet Union from attack, is as I have characterised it, we need now to revert to the status of the primary intention and, in particular, to whether such dissuasion can be legitimately regarded as the object of an intention. To assist in deciding this, let us reconsider the example of the board meeting earlier introduced. In that case also we had left undescribed how the chairman expected to fulfil his intention of persuading the board members to vote for the motion. Let us suppose that he intends to do this by inducing in them the belief that he might resign if they do not so vote, and let us further suppose that his resignation would be a signally unwelcome outcome. As thus described, his primary intention is to persuade them to vote for the motion and his secondary intention, the fulfilment of which is necessary to the achievement of the primary intention, is that they should believe he might resign if they do not vote for the motion. This would seem a perfectly legitimate characterisation of his intentions. But if so, there would appear no reason why the intentions underlying deterrence should not be similarly described. For just so do NATO political leaders intend to dissuade the Soviet Union from an attack by inducing in the Soviet leaders the belief that NATO might use nuclear weapons if attacked. The primary intention in maintaining a deterrent capability is thus to dissuade the Soviet Union from attack. And the secondary intention — the fulfilment of which is necessary to the achievement of the primary intention — is that the Soviet Union should believe that NATO might use nuclear weapons if attacked.

We have now characterised the intentions required by our political leaders for deterrence to be effective. We must now consider the position of the serviceman manning the deterrent. For it may be objected that the characterisation of the secondary intention may be appropriate for the US President or British Prime Minister but is not appropriate to the captain of the Polaris submarine. Surely he has a conditional intention to fire the missile if he receives a properly authenticated order to do so from the proper authority (i.e. ultimately the President/PM). Indeed, his readiness to obey such an order is an essential part of maintaining the deterrent in operational readiness. Thus, however attenuated and complex may be the intention attributed to our political leaders, the Polaris commander's intention is of the simpler 'if A, X' form. This is, I believe, so — but what is relevant to note is that the condition on which the implementation of his intention is dependent would only be fulfilled if the PM or President — who constitutes the proper authority from whom ultimately the order to use the weapons might come — were to form the intention to issue such an order. In that sense the Polaris commander's conditional intention is derivative of the intentional state of the PM/President. Moreover, in so far as deterrence does not require the latter to have formed such an intention, the Polaris commander's conditional intention remains 'pure', i.e. does not lead to action.

To summarise the argument so far. We started with two alternative formulations of the intention underlying deterrence both rather vaguely and implausibly attributed to NATO as a whole (implausibly, since not everyone living in NATO could reasonably be said to have such intentions). These formulations we have now seen are not alternative but complementary, although deterrence has emerged as a much more complex activity than initially assumed. Indeed, maintaining a deterrent capability involves a wide variety of actions/activities by a wide variety of people, each of whom will have different intentions underlying their actions. But for the purpose of the moral evaluation to which I now turn, I have singled out as of particular importance three kinds of intentions:

(i) The primary intention of NATO political leaders in maintaining a nuclear deterrent capability, together with NATO's conventional forces, is to dissuade the Soviet Union (or any other potential nuclear adversary) from an attack against NATO.

(ii) The secondary intention of our political leaders, the fulfilment of which is necessary to the achievement of the primary intention, is that the Soviet Union (or other potential nuclear adversary) should believe that NATO might intend to use the weapons if attacked: a position not based on bluff since our political leaders have not ruled out the option of possible use, even though they do not have a firm intention to use them.

(iii) The intention of the servicemen operating the nuclear component of the deterrent is to fire it, if they receive a properly authenticated order from the proper authority.

I shall begin the moral evaluation by considering whether it is possible to provide a justification for nuclear deterrence even if one believes that any use of nuclear weapons would be morally impermissible in any circumstance. This is the position, for example, apparently adopted by the US Catholic bishops in their recent Pastoral Letter on War and Peace.[15]

To defend this position it might be argued that the primary intention underlying deterrence is to dissuade an adversary from aggression — a morally laudable aim; nuclear weapons would be used only if deterrence fails; deterrence is a robust and valid system which will not fail; ergo, deterrence can be justified solely by reference to its primary aim.

I share much of the confidence in the likely success of deterrence assumed by this argument, although the presumption that deterrence could never fail is perhaps too strong. But, even without that defect, our earlier analysis of deterrence suggests that the argument deals too brusquely with the moral difficulties. For, as we have argued, maintaining a deterrent involves more than just the primary intention — however important that may be to the moral evaluation. It also requires that our political leaders have at least not ruled out altogether the option of possible use and that the servicemen manning the deterrent have the weapons deployed in operational readiness for use. Thus the absolute distinction pre-supposed by this argument between deterrence and use is far too simplistic.

A rather more sophisticated version of this argument might be mounted by questioning the universal validity of the moral principle that 'If it is wrong to do X it is wrong to intend to do X' — let us call this principle I.[16] This principle, it may be claimed, is normally valid since at least quite often we do what we intend to do and, indeed, this is the whole point of having the intention. But in some cases (e.g. conditional deterrent intentions) we do not do what we intend (conditionally) to do — indeed the whole point of having the conditional intention is precisely to seek to ensure that the condition, upon which fulfilment of the intention is dependent, does not come about: using our earlier terminology, such intentions are intrinsically 'pure'. In such cases the autonomous effects of having the intention are of more importance to the moral assessment than the actual act intended and its consequences. Thus, if having the intention 'to do X, if A' is very likely to secure highly beneficial effects, while it is extremely unlikely that the condition will be fulfilled, upon which is dependent performance of the presumed morally impermissible act X, it may be morally justified to have the intention.

The following example may help illustrate the point.[17] Suppose a terrorist is threatening to blow up a school full of children and by chance Smith has access to the family of the terrorist. The only way Smith can stop the terrorist blowing up the school is by telling him that, if he does it, Smith will inflict comparable damage on his children, even though Smith would regard doing this as morally impermissible. Let us further suppose that Smith has good reason to believe that the terrorist will back down in the face of such a threat (the terrorist is, for example, known to be very attached to his own family). In these circumstances we might surely conclude that Smith should make the threat. If so, we should apparently be concluding that it was morally justified to say that one intends to do what is morally impermissible because of the very probable and beneficent effects of expressing the intention and the extreme unlikelihood of carrying it out. Is not this a clear breach of principle I?

But is it? Certainly the example shows that there may be cases where it is morally justified to say that one intends to do what is morally illicit, but saying that one intends to do something and intending it are, as we have already seen, quite distinct. If Smith is simply bluffing, this will hardly breach principle I, nor will it be helpful to the defender of deterrence which, we have already argued, is not based on simple bluff. But could not Smith be said to intend to carry out the threat, particularly since — *ex hypothesi* — he knows it is very unlikely that the condition will be met, upon which implementation of the threat is dependent? I find this rather doubtful.

As noted earlier, if I intend to do X I must (logically) regard doing X as in some sense desirable and possible — let us summarise these two conditions as 'doable'. Could Smith regard as 'doable' an act which he regards as morally impermissible in any circumstances? Of course he could — he may be wicked or akratic (weak-willed). But since our only interest in this example is whether it illustrates a particular kind of moral justification, let us assume he is neither. In other words, can an agent who wishes to do only what is morally right in this situation regard an act as 'doable' which he considers to be not just wrong but morally impermissible in any circumstances? Surely he cannot and hence he cannot be said to intend to do it. Nor does it help that it is extremely unlikely that the condition will be met, upon which his performing the act is dependent, since — *ex hypothesi* — he regards the act as morally impermissible in *any* circumstance — however remote and implausible that circumstance may be.

From the fact that he cannot be said to intend to do what he is threatening, it does not yet follow that he is only bluffing since perhaps, although he does not intend to do it, he has not yet ruled out the option. But this position is surely not available to someone with such absolute moral beliefs about the action. If he regards the act as morally impermissible in any circumstance then it is the kind of act which — in so far as he wishes to act morally — he must necessarily rule out as an option. It would therefore appear that he must be bluffing. And if so, this is not relevant to nuclear deterrence.

Indeed the discussion thus far suggests that anyone who holds such absolute views on the moral impermissibility of using nuclear weapons is likely to find very considerable difficulty in providing a moral justification for deterrence. For if deterrence is to be morally justified, it would appear that the advocate of deterrence must be prepared to concede that their use might be morally justified in at least some circumstances.

To explore this position let us vary the terrorist example we have been examining. Let us suppose that the terrorist has captured Smith's home and family and is about to torture them slowly, surely and painfully to death. The only way Smith can prevent this is by threatening to blow up the house with the terrorist and Smith's family inside, unless the terrorist releases them — in which case he will be allowed to go free. Let us further consider two alternative variants:

A. that Smith's knowledge of the terrorist suggests that it is extremely likely that, if faced with such a threat, the terrorist will withdraw leaving the family unharmed (the terrorist is well known for being anxious to preserve his own neck).
B. that Smith's knowledge of the terrorist suggests that it is very unlikely that the terrorist will back down in the face of such a threat (the terrorist group to which he belongs is known for its kamikaze tactics).

Let us suppose that Smith makes the threat and is not bluffing.

If he is not bluffing then — for the reasons already adduced — he cannot regard the act as morally impermissible in any circumstance. But he would clearly regard killing his own family with acute moral horror. The difference between this example and the earlier one is that, as described, Smith might just regard the action as morally justified, however morally repugnant (the quick death from the explosion would save his loved ones from the slow anguished torture they would otherwise face). It might just be regarded as the lesser of two evils.

But what then explains the felt moral difference between variant A and variant B of this example? I suggest that this arises from the fact that since in variant A it is extremely unlikely that the condition will be fulfilled which might require him to do the act, both we as outsiders and Smith, as the agent looking at the problem from the inside, can attach more weight in the moral evaluation to the probable beneficent effects of the threat itself. Moreover, Smith need not have decided yet whether he would implement the threat, although — *ex hypothesi* — he has not ruled this out altogether as a possible option. But in variant B, since it is very unlikely that the threat will work, very little weight can be attached to the beneficent effects of the threat, while Smith is faced with a real prospect that the condition upon which implementation of the threat is dependent will be fulfilled. He cannot therefore regard implementation of the threat as just a possible option. The anguish we feel over variant B is precisely the anguish that any moral agent would feel when faced with such an appalling choice between two evils.

Do these examples breach principle I: that if it is wrong to do X, it is wrong to intend to do X? I think not. But they do suggest that, if the principle is not to suffer from fatal equivocation, it needs to be very carefully expressed. In particular, the moral terms used in both the protasis and apodosis need to be used with exactly the same force and meaning. Thus, if doing X is an act which it would be morally impermissible to do in any circumstances, it would be morally impermissible to intend to do X, even conditionally. But if doing X is an act which, although wrong *qua* involving moral harm, could be justified in the circumstances as the lesser evil, it may be morally permissible to do X and hence to intend to do X in those circumstances. Moreover, even if there is a moral presumption against doing X, it may still be licit to retain the possible option of doing X, provided doing X might in some circumstances be morally permissible and provided there are very good reasons for not excluding the option. But if doing X would be morally impermissible in any circumstances, it would be illicit even to retain the option of doing X, however strong the reasons for retaining the option.

Reverting to nuclear deterrence, our argument suggests that if deterrence is based on a firm intention to use nuclear weapons, if A — for example, if other means have failed to prevent aggression by a nuclear power — this conditional intention would only be morally permissible if the use of nuclear weapons, if A were always morally permissible: a claim which it would be very difficult to establish, in view of the moral presumption against use and the wide variety of circumstances in which the question of use, if A might arise. But our earlier analysis of the intentions underlying deterrence has suggested that the deterrent threat does not need to be backed by a firm conditional intention to use nuclear weapons nor that any such decision should have been made. It merely requires that our political leaders have not ruled out altogether the option of possible use. The retention of the option of possible use could be licit provided use — however morally repugnant and however real the moral harm caused — might in some circumstances be justified as the lesser evil and provided any manifestly ethically impermissible use has been eschewed. The one conditional intention which it would be essential to have, on moral grounds, would thus be the exclusive conditional intention: to use nuclear weapons *only* if such use were deemed ethically permissible. Moreover, in view of the moral presumption against use, such a position would only be ethically tolerable if there were very good reasons for not excluding the option of use altogether.

But the advocate of deterrence does, of course, believe there are such good reasons: the beneficent effects of the deterrent threat in dissuading an adversary from aggression. These beneficent effects could not be used to justify the deterrent threat if its implementation, however unlikely, would necessarily be morally impermissible. But it may be possible morally to justify a deterrent threat, based on the retention of the option of possible use, in view of its highly probable and beneficent effects and the extreme unlikelihood of its implementation, provided the use of nuclear weapons, in some form and circumstances relevant to deterrence, might be morally licit and provided any manifestly impermissible use has been eschewed.

It may, however, be objected that it is morally irresponsible for our political leaders not to have decided now whether or not they would authorise the use of such weapons, if other means have failed to prevent aggression by a nuclear power. To leave such a fateful decision to the heat of crisis when passions run high and time runs short is criminal irresponsibility.

Part of the answer to this objection is provided by the comparison between variant A and B of the terrorist example. Certainly it would be morally irresponsible not to have made up one's mind if it seemed likely that such aggression were imminent. But this — for the reasons advanced in Chapter 1 — the advocate of deterrence believes is a remote possibility precisely because of the beneficent effects of deterrence. The other part of the answer may require a fuller description of the moral position which it would be necessary for our political leaders to hold, if they are to avail themselves of such a moral justification of deterrence.

Of course, if they have not considered the moral difficulties involved in the use of nuclear weapons, then it would be irresponsible to defer such consideration until a crisis is upon us. Our hypothetical political leaders would, however, need to be deeply serious moral agents. They must have surveyed all the usual scenarios for use of nuclear weapons and be very alive to the moral difficulties involved. They readily appreciate, therefore, that there is a strong moral presumption against their use and that some uses — which they must have excluded — would be ethically impermissible. They are, however, not prepared to rule out that a possible morally licit use might arise in some, perhaps as yet unconceived, circumstance. They may perhaps be mindful of historical precedents and of the fact that no one in the 1920s foresaw that in the 1930s he would be faced with the monstrous evil of Nazism and that the removal of that evil would require a war — generally regarded as just — which claimed the lives of 50 million people. It is not therefore that they are unaware of the moral presumption against the use of nuclear weapons, nor are they casually leaving the decision until the heat of crisis arrives. Rather, it is precisely because they are aware of the moral presumption against use that they deem it morally irresponsible to decide in advance, and without knowing the precise circumstances in which the question of use might arise, whether or not it would be justified. But although they thus fully appreciate the moral constraints on use, they appreciate also the fact that deterrence insures against the unforeseen and that a defence policy needs to be able to cater for many changed circumstances. What they are not prepared to rule out is that circumstances could arise and, if they did, would require deep and anguished moral thought long before the crisis point was reached in which a use of nuclear weapons might be morally justified.

But if the position of the PM/President could thus be justified, what of the Polaris commander to whom we earlier attributed a firm, albeit conditional, intention to fire the missiles if he received a properly authenticated order from the proper authority? He is doing rather more than not merely ruling out an option. That is so, but — as noted earlier — his conditional intention is derivative of that of the PM/President. If we assume that the PM/President will only authorise the use of the weapons in circumstances where this is morally justified, and if we further assume that the Polaris commander has good reason to believe this to be so, then there is no reason why his conditional intention should not be morally legitimate. For the Polaris commander to have such good reason, he would need to be satisfied that the targeting and other plans related to use adequately reflected the moral constraints and, in particular, eschewed any manifestly ethically impermissible use. But these are not additional conditions that need to be satisfied for his benefit: they would need to be satisfied anyway if deterrence is to be morally licit. The only additional requirement for the Polaris commander is to know that these conditions are satisfied: that he is playing a part in an ethically justifiable deterrent system.

I thus conclude that it is not possible to provide a moral justification of nuclear deterrence, if one believes that any use of nuclear weapons would be morally impermissible. But since, to be effective, deterrence requires only the retention of the option of possible use, it may be possible to provide such a justification, in view of the beneficent effects of the deterrent threat and extreme unlikelihood of its implementation, provided use of nuclear weapons could be morally licit in some form and some circumstance relevant to deterrence.

But, in view of the grave objections to use noted in Chapter 4, can even this attenuated claim be rendered plausible? To this task we turn in the next chapter.

7 DETERRENCE AND USE: THE JUST WAR THEORY REAPPLIED

There is, I have argued, a strong moral presumption against any use of nuclear weapons, while any very large-scale use even against military targets, still more cities, would be morally forbidden. To assess whether use in some form and circumstances might none the less be morally licit, it is necessary to consider first what options for use need to be retained, if deterrence is to be effective.

It is sometimes assumed in public debate on deterrence that the stability and effectiveness of deterrence ultimately relies on the threat to use nuclear weapons in a wholesale and undiscriminating manner of precisely the kind that would be precluded by our moral argument. This is the view of deterrence, aptly labelled by the acronym MAD, that seeks to base deterrence on the threat of mutual assured destruction: a view chillingly encapsulated in the moral inversion of John Newhouse's aphorism, 'Killing people is good, killing weapons is bad.'[1] This assumption has, moreover, survived, indeed, been largely impervious to the official statements of US Government targeting policy which, as noted in Chapter 1, have, by contrast, increasingly stressed over the last decade the need for selectivity and priority to be accorded to military targets. We need, therefore, to consider whether deterrence necessarily requires, as at least its ultimate sanction, use of genocidal threats. Is deterrence, in other words, necessarily MAD?

I have argued that the conditions for stable mutual deterrence are twofold:

(i) Each side has the ability, if attacked by the other, to inflict on the attacker sufficient damage to outweigh any conceivable gain to be secured from the attack.
(ii) Neither side can rule out that the other might use this ability, if attacked.

It is necessary to concede that if the only uses one is prepared not to rule out are of the very limited kind that pose no or very little risk to non-combatants, e.g. their use in anti-submarine warfare, a demonstration shot or a single low-yield attack on a military target

87

distant from population centres, these would not suffice to meet the conditions of stable deterrence. This is not to deny that such uses could suffice to re-establish deterrence, if it were ever to fail. But they would only do so by impressing on an adversary the risk of further use, that is, by raising the spectre of escalation. It is true that, even if we had forsworn any more militarily significant use, an adversary could never be sure of this. And the uncertainty could suffice to establish deterrence. But the risk would remain that an adversary might seek to call our bluff, discerning that such a limited use was a sign of political weakness rather than of resolve to resist aggression. For the conditions of stable deterrence to be fulfilled, it appears that we must be prepared not to rule out more militarily significant use: that is, use which, although designed to operate on the political will of an adversary, does so by means of its substantive military impact.

At this point it may appear that we risk being set on a slippery slope leading inexorably to the very genocidal threats whose moral legitimacy I have eschewed. We seem faced with a 'Heads I win, tails you lose' dilemma: for deterrence to be stable we need to threaten the mass killing of non-combatants, which is immoral; selective strikes against military targets may be morally licit but are not enough to deter.

Can this dilemma be escaped? I think it can, since it poses an entirely false dichotomy. The presumption that it is only genocidal threats that deter does not derive from the logic of deterrence but rather reflects a combination of the particular historical circumstances in which the nuclear era was initiated and some deeply muddled thinking about deterrence.

Historically, nuclear weapons first appeared at the end of a long war in which city bombing had been regular practice. The success of that policy had been, of course, decidedly mixed: against Germany, in particular, area bombing had signally failed to induce surrender, much greater success having been achieved by the precision bombing of the last year of the war against military and related targets, including transportation and oil production facilities. None the less, the use of nuclear weapons against cities appeared a natural continuation and, indeed, vindication of the policy of area bombing. The failure of that policy to induce German defeat, it was suggested, derived from the fact that the bombs used were insufficiently devastating rather than from any inadequacy of the underlying theory: in particular, the crucial failure, noted in Chapter 3, to explain how damaged civilian morale was supposed to lead to the political change required to end the fighting in a totalitarian society from which all organised political opposition had been barred. Even more importantly, in the early nuclear era there was little choice but to target cities given the initial scarcity of bombs, poor intelligence and lack of any accurate means of delivery. Even when the scarcity problem was solved, the lack of accurate means of delivery persisted and was compensated for by the size of the bombs produced. 'This history', as Fred Iklé concluded, ' — not reasoned strategic analysis — led us into the habit of thinking that we had to threaten the killing of millions and millions of people to deter an "aggressor".'[2]

As regards the muddled thinking underpinning the presumption that only genocidal threats deter, this has been multifarious. In part, it reflects the fallacy that for deterrence to work it is necessary to threaten an adversary with more harm than he can do to us, whereas — as I have argued — all that is required is the ability to inflict on him sufficient damage to outweigh any conceivable gains to him of his aggression. In part, it reflects a failure to appreciate how devastating any significant use of nuclear weapons would be and that beyond certain damage levels there is, as Bernard Brodie noted, 'a curve of deterrence effect to which each unit of additional damage threatened brings progressively diminishing increments of deterrence'.[3] Finally, it also reflects some deeply confused thinking about the likely attitude of the Soviet leadership: on the one hand, the assumption that they valued their populace more than their military assets but, on the other, that perhaps they did not value their populace very much and would hence only be impressed by threats of the most dire kind. Some of this muddled thinking has been well criticised by McGeorge Bundy, former US Presidential Special Adviser for National Security Affairs:

> There is an enormous gulf between what political leaders really think about nuclear weapons and what is assumed in complex calculations of relative advantage in simulated strategic warfare. Think tank analysts can set levels of 'acceptable' damage well up in the tens of millions of lives. They can assume that the loss of dozens of great cities is somehow a real choice for sane men. They are in an unreal world. In the real world of real political leaders — whether here or in the Soviet Union — a decision that would bring one hydrogen bomb on one city of one's own

country would be recogized in advance as a catastrophic blunder.[4]

Neither genocidal threats nor threats approaching that level are thus required by the logic of deterrence, while the technology is now available, in a way that it has not been in the past, to permit a more discriminating and precise use of the weapons, even with submarines as the launch platforms. It is difficult, in the abstract and without relation to the particular circumstances of a potential aggressor, to specify precisely what threatened damage levels are needed for successful deterrence. But there is no reason why a limited damage plan could not be devised which, while eschewing counterpopulation strikes and concentrating primarily on military and related targets, particularly an adversary's conventional forces and their supporting infrastructure, was still prepared not to rule out damage levels sufficient to convince an aggressor that the costs of any aggression would amply outweigh the benefits. Indeed, such a plan would surely have a very powerfully dissuasive effect on a totalitarian regime, such as that of the Soviet Union, were it to be tempted by foreign adventure, in view of the extent to which such a regime relies upon its armed forces to assure not merely its external security but also its internal security and continued hold over sometimes reluctant satellite states.

Such a countercombatant targeting policy (so called to distinguish it from a counterforce policy directed at eliminating an adversary's nuclear forces) would thus meet the first condition of stable deterrence, by providing the ability to inflict on a nuclear aggressor sufficient damage to outweigh the gains of his aggression. It would also meet the second requirement of credibility — that the aggressor could not rule out that such a plan might be implemented — and, indeed, would do so far more effectively than a policy based on unbelievable threats of mutual genocide.

But it may still be objected that the attempt to humanise nuclear war in the way morality demands is to lapse into the kind of Ptolemaic thinking which the Copernican thought revolution necessitated by the nuclear era has, as stressed in Chapter 1, rendered outmoded. It is to attempt to render tolerable what is — and what the effectiveness of deterrence requires must remain — intolerable, by making war in the nuclear era once again appear fightable and even winnable. But is that so?

It is, indeed, a feature of what is proposed that thought should be given to what options for use should or should not be ruled out were deterrence to fail. But this refusal to regard the outbreak of nuclear war as, in Laurence Martin's phrase, 'an impenetrable veil beyond which thought and planning should not proceed'[5] is surely a virtue, not a defect. However stable and effective deterrence undoubtedly is, there is still a finite, albeit infinitesimal, chance that it might fail. It is, therefore, politically and morally irresponsible to give no thought to our possible actions were this to occur. But the fact that certain options for using nuclear weapons have not been ruled out, does not mean that they would be implemented, still less does it mean that a nuclear war could, in any way, be regarded as fightable, still less winnable.

Given the immense destructiveness of nuclear weapons, even their limited use would still be horrific and carry a risk of escalation to even more horrendous levels. A war which might involve use of nuclear weapons would be neither fightable — in the sense of worth initiating — for the costs of aggression would far exceed the gains; nor winnable, since a classical military victory would remain a chimera, given each side's inability to deprive the other of its nuclear capability. A countercombatant targeting policy would in no way detract from these two fundamental axioms of the nuclear Copernican revolution. Rather, it would give them clearer and more explicit recognition, both by eschewing any large-scale use of nuclear weapons in the doomed pursuit of military victory and by accepting that the only rational aim, were deterrence ever to fail, would be to seek to terminate the conflict as quickly as possible at the lowest possible level.

Finally, it may be objected that a countercombatant targeting policy might appear provocative to an adversary through confusion with a counterforce policy, while development of the weapon systems required to implement the policy would be inimical to arms control negotiations. The latter objection may have had some force in the past but, as has been stressed, the technology is now already available to permit implementation of such a policy. Nor is there any reason why the policy should be deemed provocative. Indeed quite the reverse. For the policy would pre-eminently not be motivated by the mistaken belief that the other side's nuclear forces could be eliminated by a disabling first or, indeed, subsequent strike. For that reason the policy would accord priority, unlike a counterforce policy, to conventional military and related targets and their supporting infrastructure. As noted in Chapter 1, the estimated 40,000 potential target installations identified in the US Single Integrated Operational Plan already include a vast range of selective countercombatant options. A countercombatant policy would therefore not require any addition to the target plan but rather a reduction in the target options: a move that could hardly be considered provocative.

A countercombatant targeting policy would thus meet the requirements of stable and effective deterrence. But the crucial question still remains whether its implementation, if the need for this were to arise, could ever be morally licit. Such a policy, by deliberately seeking to minimise non-combatant casualties, may appear vastly preferable morally to a policy based on mutual assured destruction, which seeks to maximise such casualties. But the immense destructiveness of nuclear weapons means that, however carefully targeted against military assets, substantial non-combatant casualties would result, unless the nuclear exchange could be confined to the lowest level.

It is for this reason that I have readily conceded that there is a strong moral presumption against any use of nuclear weapons. But the version of deterrence that I have sought to defend requires only that it should be permissible to retain the possible option to use nuclear weapons in some circumstances to resist aggression by a nuclear power. To refute this, it is therefore not enough to show that there is a moral presumption against use. What is required is to establish the very much stronger claim that there is no conceivable circumstance in which a militarily significant use could be morally licit.

To assess whether this very strong claim can be established we need to consider whether the two principles of the just war tradition that posed particular difficulties for nuclear weapons — those of proportion and of discrimination — would necessarily preclude any use of nuclear weapons to resist aggression.

Neither principle excludes the legitimacy of non-combatant casualties resulting from military action: the former insists, however, that the suffering caused both to combatants and non-combatants should be proportionate to the good aimed at; while the latter, in the form earlier presented, requires that non-combatant casualties should be minimised as far as possible, and that any military action which would certainly cause the deaths of non-combatants, even where these are unintended, would only be licit if this were the only way to prevent a very great harm and if the good thereby achieved would clearly and decisively outweigh the harm. Let us therefore consider the application of each of the principles to the use of nuclear weapons.

The principle of proportion would need to be applied both to the decision to resort to war to resist aggression by a nuclear power and to any use of nuclear weapons in the conduct of such a war. In so far as the principle would preclude the latter, *a fortiori* would it rule out a decision to resort to war involving commitment to such use. Let us therefore consider whether any use of nuclear weapons in the conduct of the war would necessarily cause disproportionate suffering. To some this may appear a simple and, indeed, self-evident moral truism. But it is far from being either. It is rather a complex moral judgement that itself presupposes a deal of factual argumentation.

Proportion is a relation between two magnitudes and their respective probabilities. The only use of nuclear weapons acknowledged by NATO would be to secure the political objective of dissuading an adversary from continued aggression. The suffering that would be likely to be caused would therefore need to be weighed against the contribution that the use of nuclear weapons would make towards terminating aggression and the scale and imminence of the evil thereby averted. To assume that any use would be disproportionate would thus amount to the claim that, in any and all the possible circumstances in which use might be contemplated, the suffering likely to be caused would outweigh the likely good achieved. And, in turn, this claim must presuppose either a certain view of strategic realities: in particular that the NATO policy of intra-war deterrence would never succeed and that, in the face of resistance, a nuclear aggressor would never desist from his aggression; or else it must presuppose that, even if the limited use of nuclear weapons succeeded in quickly terminating the aggression, the casualty levels caused would still necessarily be disproportionate to the good achieved. I shall assess the validity of the former presupposition in addressing the problem of escalation. Let us now consider whether it is self-evident that if the casualty levels were to run into millions, as could not be excluded even if a nuclear exchange were kept limited, they would *eo ipso* be disproportionate.

To anyone whose moral sensibility has not been calloused, contemplation of such casualty levels must appear well nigh intolerable. I have, moreover, readily conceded that there are damage levels which would, indeed, be disproportionate to any conceivable good: that it would make a mockery of our pretension to be fighting justly for a just cause to be prepared to commit genocide against another country or our own national suicide or even to contemplate damage levels approaching these. But it is not self-evident that the crossover point between proportion and disproportion must always and in all circumstances be so low as to preclude any militarily significant use of nuclear weapons. For what is crucially lacking from such a judgement is any assessment of the second term in the dyadic relation of proportionality: what, in other words, is the imminence and nature of the evil being resisted at such cost.

It is perhaps difficult to conceive of such an evil in present circumstances when we have enjoyed the benefits of peace for nearly 40 years and when the threat of subjugation by an oppressive totalitarian regime is very remote, not least because of the very success of deterrence. But to consider the possible use of nuclear weapons is precisely to consider what might happen in the very remote eventuality that deterrence were to fail. Suppose we were then faced with a nuclear-armed Hitler bent on world domination and genocide: a possibility which neither history nor the succession procedures of totalitarian regimes can entirely exclude. To avert such an evil and to prevent the suffering of innocents it would draw in its wake, quite significant damage levels might be deemed proportionate. The defeat of Hitler in the Second World War cost many millions of lives. Even if, as our discussion of area bombing has suggested, some of the suffering caused was unjustified, much was not and the strategic decisions that resulted in such suffering were none the less justified. The Russian resistance to Hitler's invasion of their territory claimed millions of lives — indeed, over a million Soviet citizens died in the siege of Leningrad alone; while the subsequent liberation of Europe by the Allied armies resulted in very substantial casualty levels among both combatants and noncombatants. But from this it is hardly self-evident that the brave citizens of Leningrad were morally obliged to cede their city without resistance, still less that the Normandy landings should never have been authorised: that the Third Reich should have been allowed to remain in triumphant occupation of Europe and, indeed, to extend its grisly tentacles to embrace the whole globe.

Let us turn now to the principle of discrimination. A countercombatant targeting policy seeks to meet the requirement to minimise non-combatant casualties by its selection of targets, weapons, means of delivery and mode of attack. But, as we have conceded, unless the exchange can be confined to the lowest level, substantial non-combatant casualties could still result. The fact that efforts had been made to reduce these would be morally important but hardly removes all moral difficulty. For if substantial civilian casualties, even though unintended, were still foreseen as inevitable, we could not evade moral responsibility for them, in so far as their occurrence would be within our control and yet consented to by us.

None the less, even an attack on a military target which would inevitably result in significant civilian casualties could still be morally licit, if there were very good reason to believe that this were the only way to prevent a very great harm and that the good thereby achieved would clearly and decisively outweigh the very real moral harm thus done. It would clearly be immensely difficult for both conditions to be met, and to have very good reason to believe they would be met, by any use of nuclear weapons. But it cannot be ruled in advance, and without knowledge of the precise circumstances in which such an appalling decision might be faced, that it would be impossible.

The argument thus far presupposes that it would be possible to keep a nuclear exchange limited and that it would not inevitably escalate beyond morally tolerable limits, thereby rendering any use, however initially limited, disproportionate and indiscriminate.

Nuclear escalation is a difficult subject, not least because of the welcome lack of any experiential data. We need, therefore, to be wary of the over-confident pronouncements of some alleged experts who, often under the motivation of a mistaken view of how deterrence works, affect to know that inexorable escalation would be inevitable not just in some but in all the wide variety of possible circumstances in which use of nuclear weapons might be contemplated: that once one nuclear weapon, however small, has been let off, all would be in a massive and spontaneous orgy of self-destruction. For in the absence of experiential data and without presupposing a mechanistic theory of human behaviour, long since jettisoned from other human sciences, such sweeping predictions about how human beings would behave in such unprecedented circumstances are unlikely to have much substance. Nor can there be any mechanical substitute, whether from simulated computer war games or any other source, for the clear thought that is essential to tackle this subject. Rather, we need to take as our guiding principle the counsel of Bernard Brodie, profferred nearly 20 years ago in what remains by far the best treatment of this subject: 'There seems no substitute for old-fashioned analysis applied with special discipline to the problem that concerns us.'[6]

The concept of escalation describes the process whereby a conflict, involving at least two participants, may intensify as each side seeks to gain comparative advantage over the other. The concept is a coinage of the nuclear era but has since been extended to cover a wide variety of competitive situations. Such intensification may occur in a purely conventional conflict. But our present interest is in the extent to which a conflict involving nuclear powers may intensify to the nuclear level and at the nuclear level.

Escalation could occur as the result of the deliberate decisions of the principal protagonists or through their loss of control. In the latter case escalation would still be the result of human decision but the decisions would be those of others (for example subordinate military commanders) and unauthorised by the principal protagonists. Escalation could be limited, i.e. kept within certain bounds, or non-limited, i.e. transgressing those bounds. There are thus four principal kinds of escalation (and, of course, multiples of these):

deliberate limited escalation;
uncontrolled limited escalation;
deliberate non-limited escalation;
uncontrolled non-limited escalation.

The only kind of escalation that could conceivably be ethically permissible would be deliberate limited escalation. The ethical problems posed by escalation thus relate to the other kinds of escalation, especially non-limited escalation, whether deliberate or uncontrolled.

First, it may be objected that if deterrence depends upon the risk of non-limited escalation, this would cast doubt upon the sincerity of the eschewal of any ethically impermissible use of nuclear weapons which I have argued would be an essential condition for an ethically tolerable deterrence. For it takes two to escalate. If deterrence, therefore, relies upon the risk of non-limited escalation, we must be counting on the fact that our political leaders might, at the critical moment, abandon ethical restraint or else be unable to exercise it through loss of control.

But if we are relying on this possibility, we must in a sense have consented to it in a way that would appear inconsistent with our having sincerely ruled out , any ethically impermissible use. Secondly, it might be argued that, even if the effectiveness of deterrence does not depend upon the risk of non-limited escalation, the risk is so high as to deprive of practical content the concept of an ethically permissible use of nuclear weapons, since any use would inevitably lead to non-limited escalation. Thus, if our political leaders are sincere in eschewing any ethically impermissible use, they would — if deterrence were to fail — not use the weapons. Deterrence would thus be entirely based on bluff in a way that — as argued in the last chapter — appears implausible. Moreover, in so far as it is not based on total bluff, it may be argued that the foreseeable high risk of non-limited escalation arising from any use renders deterrence too dangerous a business to be ethically tolerable: to adopt such a policy is to consent to a course of action that has unacceptably dangerous consequences.

Let us consider each of these objections in turn.

Does deterrence depend upon the risk of non-limited escalation? Is it only effective because of that risk? Surely not. The success of deterrence depends on the fact that neither side can rule out that the other, if attacked, might inflict on the attacker levels of damage sufficient amply to outweigh the gains of the attack: a position that requires only that the option of some measure of deliberate limited escalation should not be ruled out. Nor is the fear realistic that such a position could be undermined by an adversary's willingness to escalate the conflict to a level beyond which we are prepared to go. For that would be to make the fallacious assumption, criticised earlier, that for deterrence to work it is necessary to be able to threaten an adversary with more than he can do to us rather than — as is required — sufficient harm to outweigh the gains to him of his aggression.

Perhaps, however, the fear is that an adversary could undermine our position by threatening an attack on so large a scale as to use up the quantum of ethically permissible suffering: a threat which, if implemented, would then leave us with a choice of either surrender or transgressing our self-imposed ethical limits. The implication of this argument would thus appear to be that in the face of dire threats non-resistance is always a moral duty: a very questionable presumption. For if that were so, submission to rape under extreme duress would be a moral obligation and that is hardly self-evidently so. As I have stressed, it is not merely the likely costs of resistance that need to be assessed but also the evil to be countered.

In any case, this kind of bizarre hypothesis bears little relation to any real-life situation. For an adversary would — in real life — never know precisely how far we were prepared to go and would have to reckon on the fact, noted in Chapter 1, that a defender may well be prepared to contemplate greater levels of damage in defence of his homeland than an aggressor would consider worthwhile to secure the prize of his aggression. If an aggressor, contemplating such a strategy, were to set the level of his attack too low he would thus risk facing a devastating response; while if he set it too high he would risk destroying the prize his aggression was presumably designed to acquire.[7]

Deterrence does not, therefore, need to rely for its success upon the possibility that our political leaders might abandon ethical restraint. But, of course, a totalitarian adversary, judging others by his own ethical standards, might — however mistakenly — fear this might be the case and hence be further inhibited from aggression. But this fact would not cast doubt upon our sincerity nor would it even if we chose to exploit such fears. To the extent that we adopted the latter manoeuvre this would import some element of bluff into our position but this need not be objectionable. For it is one thing to argue, as I have done, that deterrence cannot be entirely based on bluff. It is quite another to argue that some element of bluff may be useful: indeed most strategists have always assumed this to be so.

But if deterrence does not thus depend for its effectiveness on the risk of non-limited escalation, it may still be considered that the risk is so high as either to reduce any ethically permissible deterrence to a posture of total bluff or else to condemn it as being unacceptably dangerous.

The existence of some risk of non-limited escalation has to be conceded. But such a risk is not a consequence of deterrence nor even — as would be more nearly correct — the failure of deterrence: it is rather a consequence of the discovery of the immense power of nuclear weaponry. For the risk of escalation will remain so long as conflicts can occur between powers possessed of nuclear weapons or even the nuclear know-how that could be reapplied under the stress of war. It thus poses difficulties not just for deterrence but for any currently available alternative defence policy — short of complete pacifism — in the nuclear era.

Moreover, the difficulties which escalation poses for such alternative defence postures are arguably greater than those for deterrence. For, even if the risk of non-limited escalation were considered high were deterrence to fail, such a failure is a remote possibility so long as the conditions for stable mutual deterrence are fulfilled. The absolute risk (a function of both the probability of the failure of deterrence and the likelihood, in that event, of escalation) would therefore still be very low. But, even if it were conceded that unilateral nuclear pacifism might reduce the risk of nuclear escalation were a conflict to occur, such a policy could still increase the overall risk of escalation by making conflicts more likely through undermining the conditions for stable mutual deterrence. The aim of deterrence is, of course, precisely to keep as remote as possible the occasions from which escalation might arise.

But how high is the risk of non-limited escalation were deterrence to fail? Such escalation, as noted earlier, could occur either deliberately or through loss of control. Let us consider each possibility.

Escalation requires two participants. If beyond certain damage levels, the West refused to be drawn down the spiral of mutual suicide, as any ethically tolerable version of deterrence would require, further deliberate escalation would not happen. If it is, none the less, judged that such escalation would still occur it must be assumed that not only the Soviet but our own political leaders would abandon restraint once a conflict had started: that, however sincere were our eschewal of any ethically impermissible use, we would, in practice, be unable to maintain this once fighting had started.

There are, no doubt, reasons to fear this. Certainly from the onset of a major conflict in Europe there would be strong pressures for escalation fuelled by the heat, passion and fog of war. It is, however, instructive to recall that, even amidst all the passions of the Second World War, mutual deterrence against the use of gas held firm, despite the alleged experts' predictions to the contrary and the doubtful effectiveness of the 1925 Geneva Protocol. Escalation is not a mechanistic process to the outcome of which no human agent can contribute after the initial decision. On the contrary, at each stage of the process there would be decisions to be made, risks to be weighed and strong, very strong, pressures to desist.

To suppose, none the less, that the escalatory pressures would always and in all circumstances prove irresistible is to impute a suicidal recklessness to political leaders on both sides of the Iron Curtain, the motivation for which is hard to discern. For it is to suppose that each side would continue to rain blows on the other, even though neither side could thereby deprive the other of its capacity to wield nuclear force and even though each would know that such a process, unless rapidly terminated, would lead to mutual annihilation. It seems thus rather more plausible to suppose that the pressures against escalation would prevail, even without prior acceptance by our political leaders of the ethical constraints on use, much more so with this. Thus, in the event — itself very unlikely provided the conditions of stable mutual deterrence are preserved — of a major East-West conflict, it would not go nuclear, particularly since neither side could have any rational motive for launching a strategic first strike against the other; and, even if the nuclear threshold were crossed, the conflict would remain limited: the breach of the well-established 'tradition for their non-use',[8] together with the appalling consequences of further use, shocking both combatants back to their senses.

The prospects of escalation have, moreover, to be assessed against the political environment in which conflict might occur and to take into account the likely motivation in those circumstances of the participants. Let us, therefore, suppose that fighting has broken out in Europe between NATO and Warsaw Pact forces. NATO is a purely defensive alliance and has neither the will nor the capability successfully to invade Warsaw Pact territory. There is, therefore, no rational ground for the Soviet Union to fear such invasion and every reason for NATO political leaders to ensure that the Soviet Union never makes such a misjudgement as a result of unduly provocative behaviour by the West. The Soviet Union, by contrast, has the capability to invade NATO territory, in view of its massive conventional superiority, but would have no rational motive for so doing, so long as there was any possibility that NATO might respond with nuclear weapons. Were the Soviet Union ever to launch such an unprovoked invasion of NATO territory, it could only be because they had judged that NATO would not make any effective nuclear response. If, in such circumstances, the West — rather than accept defeat — were to authorise a limited use of nuclear weapons, this would oblige the Soviet Union to realise that they had misjudged the probable balance of advantage. And it is thus not at all unlikely that the Soviet Union would then desist from their aggression since they would know that further nuclear use by them would not rob the West of its retaliatory capability nor could they rule out that this might be used, particularly since — *ex hypothesi* — the West's vital interests would be more engaged than those of the Soviet Union: for the West would be defending its very homelands and way of life.

It is sometimes argued that the Soviet Union has repeatedly made clear its lack of interest in keeping a nuclear exchange limited and it is for this reason that a nuclear exchange would necessarily become non-limited. But this argument, even if it correctly portrayed the Soviet position, is simply fallacious. For, as already observed, it assuredly takes two to escalate. In any case, the extent of the Soviet lack of interest in controlling an exchange is at least open to question.

There are, of course, many Soviet pronouncements that can be cited to the effect that, in the event of aggression by NATO, whether at the nuclear or conventional level, the Soviet Union would use nuclear weapons massively and simultaneously to secure early victory. But Soviet pronouncements are, by contrast, silent on how they would conduct themselves were they the aggressors against NATO: the only scenario for which NATO plans cater and the only one in which use of nuclear weapons by NATO could conceivably be morally licit. Moreover, there has been a growing Soviet recognition that it might be possible for a conflict to be confined to the conventional level, thereby casting doubt on their earlier pronouncements that any war with NATO would inevitably go nuclear, and that even at the nuclear level, use of nuclear weapons might be more limited and controlled than hitherto supposed.[9] Quite how such doctrinal developments are to be reconciled with the continued threats of massive retaliation is not clear; still less is it clear how such threats can be reconciled with their frequent public assertions that a nuclear war is unwinnable, nor with their espousal, following Lenin, of the Clausewitzian dictum that war is an instrument of policy. Dire threats of massive retaliation may serve the ends of policy but it is unclear that their implementation would. It is a well-established Soviet practice to use doctrinal pronouncements to further their foreign policy ends. And it is a very clear objective of Soviet policy to undermine the credibility of the West's nuclear deterrent, particularly given their massive superiority at the conventional level. This point has been well made by Raymond Garthoff: 'So long as the Soviet Union gains most by complete abstention from use of nuclear weapons, it will do nothing to encourage an alternative whereby the limited use of nuclear weapons relieves the enemy from facing a choice between a strategy of defeat and one of suicide.'[10]

The doctrinal pronouncements of Soviet politicians have, therefore, to be regarded with some caution, while the published staff college writings of military officers, even if not similarly infected with ulterior political motivation, do not necessarily reveal — any more than those of their Western counterparts — how the political leadership would actually behave in a crisis. But it is the political leadership, not the military officers, to whom the decision is firmly entrusted on whether, when and how nuclear weapons would be employed: as Major-General V. I. Zemskov has soberly observed, 'The decision to employ such devastating implements as nuclear weapons has become the exclusive prerogative of the political leadership.'[11]

There are, thus, at least some grounds for doubting whether Soviet pronouncements are necessarily the best grounds for judging their likely behaviour in the event of war. Rather more helpful may be consideration of the capabilities they have acquired (which, following the Western lead, certainly include the capability for controlled and discriminate nuclear use) and, even more, their past behaviour in confrontations with the West. Soviet rhetoric has frequently been bellicose but their behaviour has been far more cautious. They have probed for Western weakness but, whenever and wherever resistance has been encountered (for example, over Berlin or Cuba), they have readily backed off. Thus, far from showing the callous disregard towards their own and their allies' populace which the assumption that they have no interest in limiting a nuclear war would impute to them, they have acted with very considerable restraint and circumspection.

But if there are thus grounds for doubting that the risk of non-limited escalation as a result of deliberate decision is very high, the risk of such escalation occurring through loss of control remains to be considered.

In the past this has been pictured as arising from an accidental computer failure or the sudden onset of insanity in an officer manning the deterrent. Such speculations were always somewhat bizarre and have increasingly been recognised as such, given the multiplicity of checks, cross-checks and physical controls designed to prevent unauthorised use. Moreover, such 'accidental' firings could only have led to escalation if they had provoked a deliberate response from the other side. The more fashionable current supposition is therefore that inexorable escalation might arise through the breakdown of command and control systems consequent upon a nuclear exchange. Is such a breakdown an unavoidable consequence of the failure of deterrence?

Political leaders on both sides have a very strong interest in retaining control over their own nuclear forces: to suppose otherwise would be to suppose that they might regard with equanimity the destruction of their own countries as a result of the unauthorised actions of their subordinates. Moreover, it is far from clear that either side would necessarily regard it as in his interest to loosen an adversary's control over his nuclear forces. It is sometimes suggested that this might be a way of reducing an adversary's ability to wield nuclear force by preventing the orders for use getting through. But, in so far as such an attack succeeded, the attacker would then face an adversary who had lost political control over some of his nuclear forces: not a self-evidently enticing prospect; while, in so far as the attack failed to destroy all the adversary's command and controls systems — as it assuredly would — he would still have to reckon on some orders getting through and hence still face the prospect of a devastating retaliatory response. The power of nuclear weapons is such that only one or two weapons are needed to inflict very substantial damage.

But if both sides thus have a very strong interest in retaining control over their own nuclear forces and no compelling motive to loosen an adversary's control over his, there would appear no reason why arrangements cannot be framed to minimise the risk of loss of control. Both sides have built in to their command and control systems substantial flexibility and redundancy precisely to reduce this risk. It is none the less true that at intense levels of exchange no system could be totally guaranteed against disruption particularly if made the direct object of attack. But it is to beg the question at issue to assume that the conflict would inevitably escalate to such levels of intensity that the system would break down through incidental damage, while it is — as I have argued — unclear why an adversary should believe it in his interest to make command and control the direct object of attack. Moreover, even if some disruption of the system were to occur, this need not lead to loss of control. For control could still be exercised by rigid insistence on the fail-safe principle that there should be no use without specific political authorisation. Indeed, it would clearly be an essential requirement for an ethical deterrent system that such a principle should be scrupulously observed. There is therefore no reason to accept that loss of control is inevitable and every reason to ensure that the risk is minimised by further improvements to present arrangements where these may be necessary both by unilateral action and arms control measures.

I therefore conclude that deterrence does not depend for its effectiveness on the risk of non-limited escalation. The risk does, none the less, exist as an ineluctable fact of the nuclear era which other defence postures than deterrence have also to face. Since it exists it does thus, inevitably, help to reinforce deterrence, while at the same time adding powerfully to the moral presumption against use. But the risk is very far from inevitable even if deterrence were to fail, while the whole aim of deterrence is precisely to keep as remote as possible occasions from which escalation might arise. The risk is therefore not so high as to render deterrence too dangerous a policy to be ethically acceptable. Still less can it be shown that the risk would always and in all circumstances be so great as to deprive of application the concept of an ethically permissible use of nuclear weapons. It would, however, need to be assessed very carefully in the light of the actual circumstances — which could vary enormously — in which use might be contemplated.

There is an immense moral presumption against any use of nuclear weapons. But it is not possible to establish in advance that there are no conceivable circumstances in which use, in some form, might be morally licit. And this minimal concession is all that is required for the version of deterrence that I have sought to defend. For this requires only that the option of use to resist aggression by a nuclear power should not be ruled out altogether. The objective in retaining the option is, however, to keep as remote as possible the circumstances in which use might arise: to ensure that the conditions for stable mutual deterrence are fulfilled and that the weapons remain rationally unusable. And it is only because deterrence thus helps to prevent war and nuclear use that it can be justified.

8 SOME POLICY IMPLICATIONS OF THE MORAL ARGUMENT

We have thus reached the conclusion that it may be possible to justify deterrence. But the force of the moral argument that we have developed does not leave deterrence entirely unscathed. In this chapter I shall explore some of the possible policy implications of the moral argument.

There is an immense moral presumption against the use of nuclear weapons. It may therefore be considered that this should be more clearly and publicly reflected in NATO policy. Prima facie, one obvious way of achieving this would be the adoption by NATO of a policy never to be the first to use nuclear weapons, as has been urged in recent years by various commentators.[1]

NATO is a purely defensive alliance whose policy is that none of its weapons — nuclear or conventional — should ever be used except in response to attack. Moreover, even in response to aggression, NATO does not have a policy to use nuclear weapons first. On the contrary, the whole aim of flexible response, as outlined in Chapter 1, would be to stop aggression as quickly as possible at the lowest possible, i.e. pre-nuclear, level. None the less, NATO policy does not exclude the possible option of first use, if this were the only way to prevent the loss of its homelands, in the face of successful conventional aggression.

At the minimum, a no-first-use policy would therefore require NATO to forgo that option. This could be done by a private decision undisclosed to the public. But advocates of a no-first-use policy have normally urged that there should also be a public declaration by NATO of the policy. Such a declaration has, of course, already been made by the Soviet Union in its statement to the UN Second Special Session on Disarmament on 15 June 1982. As a further step, a reciprocal declaration by both NATO and the Warsaw Pact might therefore be embodied in a formal treaty. Moreover, some advocates of a no-first-use policy have recognised that it would need to be accompanied and, indeed, preceded by changes in NATO's military posture. For example, the former US Secretary for Defense, Robert McNamara, who has been one of the chief advocates of a no-first-use policy, has recommended a number of such measures that would need to be taken.[2] These include: further strengthening of NATO's conventional forces; the reduction of NATO's theatre nuclear stockpile to a level required solely for retaliatory purposes — which he assesses at 'no more and probably less than 3000 weapons',[3] together with the elimination of shorter-range battlefield nuclear weapons designed primarily for early use; and the creation of a nuclear-free zone on either side of the European border, beginning in the central region.

Such measures might help lend credibility and coherence to a no-first-use policy, but they are not its distinguishing features. For similar measures would also be required by a no-early-use policy and, indeed, to an extent are already NATO policy. Thus NATO has already accepted, at least in principle, the need for increased conventional defence, as evidenced, for example, by the 3 per cent target for annual real increases in defence expenditure endorsed by the 1979 Summit. NATO has taken steps to reduce its theatre nuclear stockpile. In 1981 NATO withdrew 1,000 nuclear warheads from its European stockpile; on 26 October 1983, NATO Defence Ministers, meeting at Montebello, agreed a further unilateral reduction from 6,000 to 4,600 warheads to be implemented over the next five to six years. Once achieved, the NATO theatre nuclear stockpile will have been reduced by more than one third of its 1966 level. Thus the distinctive feature of a no-first-use policy is the intention never to use nuclear weapons first, together with, in most versions of the policy, a public declaration to this effect.

The attraction of such a policy is that it would provide a clear public expression of the moral presumption against use which might be considered of value both in itself and because of the reassurance it would give to the public in the Western democracies that NATO's deterrent policy was morally responsible. Even more importantly, it has been argued that such a public declaration would reduce the risk of nuclear war by keeping the threshold between nuclear and any other kind of conflict as wide as possible. It would, moreover, achieve this aim more effectively than a no-early-use policy by admitting of no exception. Indeed, the Soviet Union has claimed that a reciprocal declaration would not merely reduce but eliminate the risk of nuclear war. The Soviet publication *Whence the Threat to Peace?* puts it thus: 'Clearly if there is no first nuclear strike there would be no second or third strike. This would naturally make absurd all talk about the possibility or impossibility of victory in a nuclear war — the question of nuclear war would fall away altogether.'[4]

If this were indeed the consequence of a reciprocal no-first-use declaration by NATO and the Warsaw Pact, then the West should clearly match the Soviet declaration as soon as possible with one of its own. But a key question that has to be addressed in assessing the value of such declaratory postures is whether or not they would be believed. The Soviet no-first-use declaration made on 15 June 1982 has so far led to no change in NATO's perception of Soviet policy. It must, therefore, be at least open to doubt whether any similar declaration by NATO would be believed by the Soviet Union, even if it were accompanied, not, as was the Soviet declaration, by a relentless build up of theatre nuclear forces with no clear change in the tactics for their use, but by reductions and the other changes in military posture urged by McNamara.

Part of the difficulty is that intentions, even if embodied in treaties, are hard to verify and can change rapidly if circumstances change; while a no-first-use intention might appear particularly vulnerable to pressures for change, if the alternative to such use were conventional defeat. Thus it may be considered that neither side could rule out that the other — however sincere its peacetime protestations — might not resurrect the nuclear option, if faced with the prospect of such defeat. Moreover, none of the accompanying changes in military posture would guarantee the inviolability of the intention. Even a much reduced theatre nuclear stockpile, retained solely for retaliatory purposes, could still be used first; while a nuclear-free zone could be breached either by the use of longer-range systems or the reintroduction of shorter-range systems in time of crisis. But if a Western declaration were not believed, it would have no significant effect on likely Soviet behaviour and might thus give only the illusion, rather than the substance, of enhanced security.

Let us now consider the implications if a Western no-first-use declaration were believed. Would this make nuclear war less likely? It is arguable that the reverse would be the case. For the second of the two conditions for stable mutual deterrence — which required that neither side could rule out that the other might use his nuclear capability in the event of attack — would no longer hold in relation to attacks below the nuclear level. The use of conventional military force against the direct interests of a nuclear power might, therefore, once again, become a rational option, for the costs of such aggression might no longer seem prohibitively high.

This is, moreover, a particularly worrying prospect for NATO, given the massive preponderance which the Soviet Union enjoys at the conventional level, including a major chemical weapon capability. The Soviet Union might be more tempted to exploit its conventional superiority, if it really believed that the West would never resort to nuclear weapons, particularly since the Soviet ability to mount such an attack would be enhanced by the removal of the need to disperse its forces to reduce their attraction as a nuclear target: close massing of Soviet forces to achieve a conventional breakthrough would thus be facilitated. The resulting conventional conflict, fought on the densely-populated territory of central Europe, would — as has been frequently stressed — be a deeply devastating event, even if confined to the conventional level, while the risk would remain that such a conflict could escalate to the nuclear level, whether through the use of nuclear weapons by the aggressor to overcome successful conventional opposition or by the defender, about to be overborne by a successful conventional attack, reinstating the nuclear option rather than accept the loss of his homelands. Given the potential horror of modern conventional war and the risk of nuclear escalation from the first conventional shot, the decisive boundary line that has to be preserved is between peace and war. But a no-first-use declaration, by appearing to reduce the costs of war, might make the breach of that boundary line more likely and, far from reducing, might thus increase the risk of conventional and, hence, nuclear conflict.

Some of these difficulties could no doubt be lessened if the West were — as some advocates of no first use have urged — to take measures to remove or at least substantially to reduce the conventional imbalance, so that the West could offer a more prolonged conventional resistance than the few days or weeks currently assumed. But even if achievable, this could still not guarantee that a conventional attack could never appear a rational option to an aggressor for, as argued in Chapter 1, conventional deterrence is inherently less stable than nuclear deterrence, since even the costs of failure are not necessarily prohibitively exorbitant. Nor could a defender, however robust his conventional capability, ever be completely confident that his conventional defence would succeed and that he would never be faced with the alternative of surrender or nuclear use.

In any case, it must be doubtful whether the conventional imbalance could ever be completely removed. No doubt misleading statistics are sometimes quoted on the extent of the imbalance. The imbalance certainly looks worse if attention is concentrated on in-place forces in the European theatre rather than on global comparisons. But to say this is not to deny the imbalance but rather to place it in its geographical perspective. In part, it reflects the ineluctable facts of geography: that the major partner in the Western Alliance is separated from Europe by the Atlantic Ocean, whereas the USSR is itself a European power. Reinforcements to Western Europe from North America would thus have to travel 6,000 kilometres; it is only 650 kilometres from the western borders of the USSR.

To nullify this geographical imbalance would require a massive and almost certainly politically unrealistic increase in the European defence effort, together with a substantial pre-positioning in Europe of American equipment and men, the political viability of which — from both an American and European viewpoint — is open to doubt. The risk would, moreover, remain that such efforts could merely provoke a futile arms race, with the Soviet Union further building up its conventional forces in order to retain its superiority.

A more fruitful solution might therefore appear to be, not to seek to build up to equality, but to build down to it by negotiating a reduced common ceiling of in-place forces in Europe. This has been the aim of the Mutual Balanced Force Reduction negotiations in Vienna since their inception in 1973. But the halting progress of these negotiations offers no early prospect of success. Moreover, although a reduced common ceiling, if achieved, would represent a major gain, it would still not remove the problems stemming from the geographical imbalance. For it would always be open to the USSR massively to reinforce its force levels in time of crisis, a task which it could accomplish far more readily than the West, in view of its geographical position.

A public no-first-use declaration by the West would therefore, at best, if not believed, make little difference to Soviet perceptions and, at worst, if believed could increase the risk of war by weakening deterrence. In view of these disadvantages, the attraction of such a policy is much reduced. It might, however, still be held that such a policy would have merit, if it were not publicly disclosed. The West would, thus, firmly decide never to use nuclear weapons first but would not publicly announce this decision and, indeed, in the interests of maintaining the conditions for stable mutual deterrence might even encourage the Soviet Union to believe the opposite. Our defence posture would thus include an element of bluff but this need not count decisively against it. For, as argued in the last chapter, even if deterrence cannot be entirely based on bluff, some element of bluff may be acceptable.

What would be the advantages of such a secret posture? It would no longer provide the clear public expression of the moral presumption against use nor the resulting reassurance for domestic audiences. An intention that cannot be publicly disclosed might also appear even more vulnerable to change in changed circumstances than a publicly avowed intention, the breach of which would at least damage one's international reputation and credibility. It might, none the less, still be considered that such a posture would bring about some reduction in the risk of nuclear conflict. It would not remove that risk since, quite apart from the possibility that the intention might be changed under the pressures of a failing conventional defence, nuclear use could always be initiated by an aggressor to press home his attack. But the refusal of one participant to initiate nuclear use could still reduce the risk of the nuclear threshold being crossed. The converse of this position is, however, that its holder would be obliged to concede to an adversary whatever gains he could secure by aggression using conventional, including chemical, weapons in any and all the circumstances in which such aggression might occur. Thus, if thereby faced with the choice of the loss of one's homelands to a ruthless totalitarian aggressor or surrender, one should always choose surrender. In view of the moral presumption against use this might be the only morally tenable course of action. But to suppose that it must always, and in all circumstances, be our moral duty is to presuppose that the moral difficulties attendant upon first use must always be overriding in a way that they are not for second use. And that would appear mistaken.

The immense moral presumption against use applies as much to second and subsequent use as to first, while, in so far as any use could be licit, there would seem no reason why first use should always be precluded in a way that second is not. For both the internal quality of the action and the external effects of first or second use need not differ significantly. Second use could cause as much suffering of innocents as first and carry a similar risk of escalation. Moreover use — whether first or second — would be undertaken by NATO with precisely the same intention: to persuade a nuclear aggressor to desist from his aggression. Indeed, it is perhaps arguable that, if there is any significant moral difference, the difficulties might be less for first use than second in so far as first use might offer a better prospect of success: for an aggressor who had launched an attack on the calculation that the use of nuclear weapons could be avoided would be very rapidly obliged to reappraise his judgement in the event of their use.

The conviction that second use is somehow less morally culpable does, none the less, persist and is perhaps attributable to one of two reasons.

First, there appears an uncritical assumption that the retaliatory use of weapons is morally less objectionable. There is, indeed, a sense in which this is correct. The use of force in response to aggression is less morally culpable than its use for aggression. As we have seen, the just war tradition would unequivocally and always condemn the latter, while conceding that the former might sometimes be justified. But this distinction is not relevant to the present case. NATO is pledged never to use any of its weapons except in response to attack. Thus, even if NATO were to use its nuclear weapons first, this would be in response to aggression. The distinction between the use of force for aggression and defence rests not on who fires first but on who commits the first act of aggression. If this were not so, Hitler's claim that Poland started the Second World War by opening fire on the German troops invading its territory might have had some plausibility.[5]

Thus, although there is a sense in which the retaliatory use of force is morally preferable, this would not appear relevant to the present issue. But the only other sense that can be attached to this claim would appear, if relevant, morally very dubious: for it would be to hark back to a pre-New Testament morality of revenge. This would be the suggestion that the retaliatory use of force was justifiable as an expression of the basic human lust for revenge: to mete out to an adversary, in Churchill's words, 'the measure and more than the measure that he has meted out to us'.[6] No doubt this is a basic human emotion but it is one that it has generally been considered the function of morality, particularly Christian morality, to curb rather than license. Moreover, the especial moral dubiety of such a retributivist position in the nuclear era has been well expressed by George Kennan:

Let us suppose there were to be a nuclear attack of some sort on this country and millions of people were killed or injured. Let us further suppose that we had the ability to retaliate against the urban centers of the country that had attacked us. Would you want to do that? I wouldn't . . . I have no sympathy with the man who demands an eye for an eye in a nuclear attack.[7]

The second reason why some have supposed that graver moral difficulties attend upon first use reflects, I suspect, a particular view of the nature of escalation as some kind of automatous spontaneous process. If escalation is a mechanistic process to the outcome of which no human agent can contribute after the initial decision, then all blame does, indeed, attach to the initiator of the process: the rest are merely puppets playing out their predetermined roles. But this view of the nature of escalation is, as argued in the last chapter, profoundly mistaken. Escalation is a process that involves at least two participants; and at each stage of the process there would be crucial decisions to be made by each participant. He who fires second cannot evade moral responsibility simply because he is second. If, in the circumstances in which use might be contemplated, the risk of unlimited escalation were assessed as so high as to preclude any morally licit use, second use would be forbidden quite as much as first.

A no-first-use policy would therefore not represent a decisive moral gain. The moral difficulties attendant upon use apply as much to second as to first use, while a public commitment to such a policy could increase the risk of war by weakening deterrence.

But even if a no-first-use policy is not the answer, the immense moral presumption against use remains, as does the need for this to be clearly and unequivocally reflected in NATO policy. This would, therefore, suggest that, at the least, NATO should firmly espouse a policy of no early use, clearly reserving such formidable armaments for use, if at all, only in the last resort.

To an extent this is already NATO policy since the aim of the Alliance would be to stop aggression at the lowest possible level and, as noted earlier, significant steps have been taken in recent years to enhance its capability to achieve this. None the less, continued and sustained efforts are required to keep the nuclear threshold as high as possible. In turn, this would suggest the need for further reductions in NATO's already reducing theatre nuclear stockpile, including the complete elimination of shorter-range battlefield systems (such as nuclear artillery shells and atomic demolition munitions) which, if usable at all, are only usable early: otherwise, they risk being overrun by an advancing enemy, in view of the need for their forward deployment. Further measures are also required to strengthen NATO's conventional capability, for it is the capacity for conventional resistance that primarily determines the level of the nuclear threshold.

A significant contribution towards this may, moreover, be possible by exploiting new technology, including some of the techniques that have permitted the more discriminating and precise use of nuclear weapons.[8] Recent developments in areas such as surveillance and target acquisition systems and precision and terminally guided munitions and submunitions offer the prospect of substantial improvements in the Alliance's ability rapidly to locate and identify distant targets and to hit them with greater accuracy and lethality using conventional weapons. This may, thus, enable conventional weapons to undertake some of the roles of shorter-range battlefield nuclear weapons. At the same time, NATO is developing tactics to exploit the new technology to enable the Alliance to undertake a more robust conventional defence by, for example, attacking Warsaw Pact reinforcements before they reach the battle zone. The combination of new technology and tactics may thus permit a significant enhancement of NATO's conventional capability. But technology is, of course, not a panacea. The technological innovativeness of the West is one of its strengths but the Soviet Union has shown itself well able to amend its own tactics to counter such changes and — sooner or later — to catch up the technological lead. Sustained improvements in other less glamorous but equally important areas, such as manpower and war stocks, are also required to increase the staying power of NATO's conventional forces.

Apart from adoption of a no-early-use policy, the force of the moral argument also imposes other constraints on the type of deterrence that may be ethically permissible. The implications for targeting doctrine of the kind of countercombatant targeting policy that I have suggested might be ethically permissible have been addressed in the last chapter. Such a countercombatant targeting policy would, moreover, permit — and the moral constraints that led to its adoption would require — reductions in the West's strategic nuclear stockpile, although with priority continuing to be given to the invulnerable submarine-launched systems. Such measures should include the elimination of multi-megaton weapons, very few, in any case, now retained by the West, whose use could only be disproportionate and indiscriminate. This would thus continue the trend already embarked on by the West, as noted in Chapter 1, but as yet only partially emulated by the East, of substantially reducing the destructive potential of its nuclear arsenal.

Finally, the moral presumption against any use imposes an obligation on both sides to negotiate deep cuts in their nuclear arsenals: a need recognised, but as yet unfulfilled, in the Western proposals in the strategic arms reduction talks (START). The many thousands of weapons held by each side are vastly superfluous to the needs of stable mutual deterrence, even taking into account the essential requirement to preserve an assured capability to inflict unacceptable damage, even after sustaining an attack. Such superfluous stockpiling is both wasteful of resources and does little to help reassure public confidence in deterrence since it appears to suggest a lack of faith in the validity of the conditions for stable mutual deterrence. It is thus open, however unjustifiably, to misrepresentation by opponents of deterrence as betokening hidden plans to fight and win a nuclear war, even though such concepts can have no application in the nuclear era and play no part in NATO plans. The counter-argument that somehow more must be better reflects pre-nuclear thinking and overlooks both the immense destructiveness of even a few nuclear weapons and the cardinal fact of deterrence that its effectiveness depends not on the ability to inflict more harm on an aggressor than he can do to us but sufficient harm to outweigh any gains to him of his aggression. Moreover, the further suggestion that nuclear superfluity, even if it confers no military advantage, may still confer a symbolic political advantage is difficult to sustain. For it is unclear who is supposed to be impressed by such bizarre arithmetic. This can hardly be third parties, whose nuclear capability, even if it exists, would still be vastly inferior to even a deeply cut superpower arsenal. But nor is there any plausible reason why the other superpower should somehow be additionally deterred by such overkill capacity, any more than would a potential criminal by a judicial threat to hang him twice rather than once.

The force of the moral argument thus requires that the West should reduce its reliance on nuclear weapons. In part, this can be achieved by unilateral action since NATO force levels need to be determined by what is required to fulfil our defence plans and do not therefore necessarily need to mirror those of an adversary: a fact long acknowledged by NATO, as evidenced, for example, by the unilateral action taken to reduce its theatre nuclear stockpile. But bilateral and multilateral action is also required, since the aim must be to reduce the nuclear arsenals of both sides to the minimum level required to ensure that the conditions for stable mutual deterrence are fulfilled. And, in so far as negotiations to attain this can only succeed with improved political relations between the superpowers, the achievement of this must be the first priority. But although morality thus requires the West to reduce its reliance on nuclear weapons, it does not require us to forgo the nuclear option altogether, at least so long as the Eastern bloc retains its weapons.

9 CONCLUSIONS AND A VISION FOR THE FUTURE

Nuclear weapons exist. They cannot be disinvented. And yet their use would be an appalling moral catastrophe. To ensure that they are never used must therefore be the objective of any ethically tolerable policy. But this is not the only objective that we have nor the only objective sanctioned by the just war theory. Over the centuries the West has developed a system of government and way of life, derived from the confluence of the classical tradition of democracy and freedom of thought with the moral and religious insights of the Judaeo-Christian tradition: a way of life that we wish to preserve and which is worth preserving. In framing a defence policy we therefore necessarily have a twofold objective: to prevent war and, in particular, the use of nuclear weapons, while at the same time preserving our political independence and way of life.

Deterrence seeks to achieve both objectives by making a virtue of necessity. Since the nuclear genie has been released from the bottle, deterrence seeks to enlist the genie in the service of peace by exploiting the awesome nature of the weapons. It uses the fear of war to prevent war; the exorbitant costs of aggression in the nuclear era to ensure that aggression does not happen and that we are left in peace to enjoy our own variegated conception of the good life.

Deterrence thus successfully capitalises on the unlovely qualities of nuclear weapons. But it is from these very qualities that the moral difficulties derive: for the appalling destructiveness of the weapons is such as to render them virtually unusable by a moral agent.

It is sometimes suggested that the moral difficulties inherent in deterrence need occasion little concern provided we are clearly moving away from deterrence, as some have claimed was the goal of the *détente* process of the 1960s and 1970s: that, although deterrence is morally impermissible as a permanent abode, it may be tolerable as a temporary resting place. And so perhaps it could be, provided only that we could see clearly an alternative and better position to which we could move within a relatively short timescale. The problem that we face — as true in the 1960s and 1970s, as in

116

the 1980s — is that no such alternative appears in sight.

Unilateral nuclear disarmament could be achieved relatively speedily but offers no reliable prospect of securing our political liberty and independence, nor yet of reducing the risk of war and nuclear use. The resumption of *détente* and achievement of substantial bilateral and multilateral arms reductions are, as argued in the last chapter, both possible — given the will to succeed on both sides — and desirable. But although the reduction in the superpowers' nuclear arsenals to the minimum level required for stable and effective deterrence is relatively easy to envisage, the step beyond to zero nuclear capability is far more difficult. For not only would each side need to be assured that the other had complied and would continue to comply with the elimination of its capability, it would also need to be assured that other nations would renounce and never seek to acquire or re-acquire such a capability. It is difficult to see how reliable assurances to this effect could be achieved without radical changes in present global political relationships nor how, without these, the mere physical removal of the weapons would necessarily enhance world security.

But if we appear thus stuck with deterrence for the foreseeable future, it is not possible for deterrence to be so divorced from use that we can enjoy the beneficent effects of the deterrent threat without having to face the moral difficulties over use. For such a position would have ultimately to be based on a gigantic bluff: a base too fragile on which to rest our security for all the, perhaps lengthy, time that deterrence may be required.

We have, therefore, been driven ineluctably by the logic of the argument to seek to fashion a version of deterrence which, while accepting the moral presumption against use, neither reduces deterrence entirely to bluff nor yet requires of our political leaders a morally impermissible conditional intention to use the weapons. We have suggested that deterrence can be effective, provided the option of use has not been entirely excluded and could be morally licit, provided use in some form and circumstances might be permissible and provided it is only such use the option of which has not been ruled out. But the only justification for retaining the nuclear option is because this appears the only way at present available of ensuring that the weapons are never used and that we can continue to enjoy the benefits of both peace and freedom. Deterrence is thus justified not because it is free of moral difficulty but because it faces less difficulty than any other currently available position.

None the less, a world freed of nuclear weapons would be a vastly preferable abode, if only it could be achieved without increasing the risk of war and without requiring readiness to surrender our independence to a hostile and alien power. There is no immediate prospect of realising such a vision, but let us finally consider whether it is necessarily for ever unattainable.

I shall begin my examination of this question not by a projection forward into the visionary future but by stepping back into the relatively recent past when — for a brief moment — it appeared that it might be possible to abolish nuclear weapons. The year was 1946 when Bernard Baruch presented to the newly formed United Nations the US Government's proposals, supported by the governments of the United Kingdom and Canada, for the abolition of nuclear weapons. Viewed after nearly 40 years of intermittent cold war and the failure of innumerable disarmament plans, it is tempting to suppose that the Baruch Plan was never more than a clever US propaganda ploy. But the evidence suggests that President Truman believed the plan had some hope of success. In the immediate aftermath of Hiroshima and Nagasaki there was a widespread and genuine conviction that, as Truman announced in his message to Congress of 3 October 1945: 'the release of atomic energy constitutes a new force too revolutionary to consider in the framework of old ideas'.[1]

The Baruch Plan proposed the creation of an international atomic development authority to which would be entrusted all phases of the development and use of atomic energy, starting with the raw materials and including:

a. Managerial control or ownership of all atomic energy activities potentially dangerous to world security.
b. Power to control, inspect and license all other, i.e. peaceful, atomic activities.
c. The duty of fostering the beneficial uses of atomic energy.
d. Research and development responsibilities to put the authority in the forefront of atomic knowledge and thus to enable it to comprehend and, therefore, to detect misuses of atomic energy.
e. The power to penalise infringements, exercised on the basis of a majority vote and not subject to veto.

Once these safeguards had been established, nuclear weapons would be banned from all national armouries.

The plan failed. And it failed because the Soviet Union objected to virtually every aspect. They believed that it gave an unfair advantage to the US since it would — necessarily — have left the US with the knowledge of how to make the weapons, a knowledge of which the plan would deprive the Soviet Union. They were fearful that their exploitation of atomic energy even for peaceful purposes would be inhibited by an authority which, in their view, would be dominated by Western interests. They objected to the inspection proposals, particularly since these provided not merely for periodic inspections of declared facilities but also empowered the authority to seek out clandestine activities. And finally, the Soviet Union objected to the proposal that the punishment of infringements should not be subject to veto.

With the benefit of hindsight, the Soviet objections are entirely predictable. What is surprising is that the plan was put forward at all. For its implications were far reaching. It would have been the first time in history that a nation (the US) had voluntarily lain down a weapon which had not been rendered obsolete by subsequent developments and of which it had an — albeit temporary — monopoly. Moreover, the proposed method of abolition would have constituted a major step towards world government. For an international atomic development authority entrusted with the power, not subject to veto, to punish infringements — Baruch's own personal contribution to the plan — would have constituted a decisive move towards a supranational security agency. And that was a radical departure from the principles on which every other operation of the United Nations was founded.

The United Nations was not envisaged as an incipient world government. It was, rather, a forum for collective action by sovereign states to promote their mutual security: a continuation and extension of the grand alliance against Hitler into the post-war world. Moreover, the reservation to the permanent members of the Security Council of the right of veto precluded such action being taken against one of the great powers: a fact that reflected both their pre-eminent position in the United Nations at its inception and the recognition that nations would never be willing to entrust to the United Nations sufficient strength to wage successful war against a major power. The Baruch proposals went far beyond mere collective security arrangements and constituted a step towards world government.

But, as rapidly became apparent, the world was not ready for such a major step. The Baruch Plan has often been criticised because it was too far ahead of its time, particularly as regards Baruch's own proposal that its enforcement powers should not be subject to veto and would hence be usable against any recalcitrant nation, including a major power. It is, however, difficult to see how the Baruch Plan or any modern equivalent could succeed with less powers, particularly as regards inspection and enforcement. For, however thorough and effective the inspection procedures, the risk of cheating would remain and, indeed, would now be far greater in view of the widespread diffusion, for civil purposes alone, of atomic energy facilities and fissionable material.

It is rather more plausible to argue that the Baruch Plan failed not because it was too radical but because it was not radical enough. It failed to tackle the root of the problem as to why nations have arms. Nations do not distrust each other simply because they have arms. Rather they have arms because they distrust each other. And it was precisely upon that lack of trust that the Baruch Plan foundered. It failed because nations distrusted each other and because of that distrust were unwilling to surrender such a key aspect of their sovereignty as the control of the most potent force ever produced to a supranational authority, itself composed of other nation-states. Only if that distrust could be removed or at least substantially reduced would Baruch or any modern equivalent plan have any prospect of success.

How then can that distrust be removed? It is sometimes argued that the distrust is a necessary concomitant of the insecurity engendered by the anarchical system of sovereign states, each pursuing its own ends in a way that inevitably — sooner or later — leads to clashes of interest. If states were abolished, so would be the need for arms and hence the risk of their use in war.

There is a trivial, because tautological, sense in which the abolition of states would abolish war. If war is defined as a conflict between states, then the abolition of states would, *eo ipso*, abolish war. But this verbal manoeuvre accomplishes nothing. Conflicts of similar intensity and violence could still continue between different groups of people: the name might be changed but not the nature of the problem. For the grounds of conflict derive not from the state system but rather from the fallen nature of man: his greed, his selfishness, his vaunting ambition. If man's moral nature could be transformed, then the problem of war and hence of nuclear weapons would, indeed, disappear.

Such a transformation is part of the Christian vision. But its realisation may seem too remote a prospect to offer any credible solution to the pressing problem of war. It may, moreover, appear unnecessary. National politics, in Kenneth Waltz's phrase, 'is the realm of authority, of administration and of law. International relations is the realm of power, of struggle and accommodation.'[2] It may, therefore, be suggested that, just as violence between individuals has been brought under control by the establishment of the state system, without any fundamental change in man's nature, so could violence between states by the institution of some form of supranational government. There is, of course, a crucial disanalogy between states and individuals since the readiness of individuals to acquiesce in the normative mechanisms of the state reflects, in part, the fact that men are approximate equals by nature and few, if any, could expect in a state of nature to prey upon their fellows for long with impunity: conditions not necessarily fulfilled in the international realm where there are marked inequalities of power, only partly mitigated by the ability of states to join together in co-operative ventures. None the less, it may be argued that a similar motivation to that which impelled men to exchange the insecurity and endless feuding of the state of nature for the order and tranquillity imposed by civil government within the state, should impel men, acting only in their rational self-interest, to exchange the present system of international anarchy for one of international order. Such motivation should, moreover, be particularly compelling now that the cost of inter-state conflict has inflated to such potentially unaffordable levels.

Thus, just as within states order is imposed by the establishment of the machinery of justice and law enforcement, so could this be achieved internationally by the institution of a supranational authority that would preside over the external relations between states. The authority would provide arbitration machinery for settling disputes between nations without the need for resort to arms and would have the power both to enforce the resulting settlements and, above all, to ensure that no nation transgressed the fundamental rule of international law forbidding aggression against each other's territory and interests. Moreover, pursuing the state analogy, the international authority would need to wield a monopoly of force in international affairs: both nuclear and conventional armaments would be banned from national authorities, except in so far as some minimal conventional force level (the amount presumably to be determined by the supranational authority) was required solely for internal security purposes. The combination of conventional and nuclear disarmament would also help reduce the danger that a ban on nuclear weapons alone could merely render the world once again safe for major conventional war, with all its own horrors and attendant risks of nuclear escalation.

Such a vision might seem to offer the prospect of a better way of ordering the relations between states. But would it? As the failure of the Baruch Plan demonstrates, the imposition of a supranational authority upon the world as it is, is hardly likely to command the assent of sovereign states. For let us suppose that the world remains as it is: that is, riven by ideological, political, tribal and cultural rivalries and marred by gross inequalities in the distribution between nations of the earth's resources. In such a world the causes for conflict would still abound and the use of force might not always seem disadvantageous, particularly in view of the disparities of power between states. A supranational authority, entrusted to enforce the peace, would need to be vested with very substantial coercive power and the occasions on which such power were exercised would be likely to be frequent. But the question then immediately arises as to why nations, even if they are prepared to forgo such advantages as their own exercise of force might secure, should trust such a supranational authority to exercise its monopoly of force wisely. The fear, not unjustifiably, would persist that the supranational authority might become a new super tyranny. Far from abolishing wars, its so-called police actions could be as brutal and savage as any inter-state conflict. Far from providing an alternative and better way of securing our political liberty and way of life, it might constitute a new and irresistible threat to them.

The risk that a supranational authority — remote from the people whose destiny it controlled and yet entrusted with massive coercive power — would degenerate into a 'soulless despotism' was clearly perceived by Kant in his pamphlet on *Perpetual Peace*.[3] For this reason he rejected the use of coercion to sustain the inter-national order for which he longed. His own recipe for inaugurating the peace, indeed to be perpetual, was, therefore, that nations should voluntarily join together to abjure the use of force to interfere in each other's affairs: to establish a *foedus pacificum* —

a peace-making federation — that, unlike an ordinary peace treaty, would be designed not to end one war, but all wars and to which all nations would eventually subscribe, as they perceived the benefits of enhanced security and economy that it provided for its members.[4] But although the respect for law without any enforcing mechanism is what makes Kant's scheme attractive, it is also its fatal weakness. It is logically necessary that if all nations are to obtain the benefit of never being attacked, all must abstain from attack. But it is logically possible for any individual nation to reap the benefits of others' abstention from force, without forswearing the use of force itself: to secure the rewards of the peace-making federation without paying its due. Since Kant eschews any supranational mechanism to enforce the terms of the federation, he has no solution to offer to such parasitic action other than the very self-help system from which he started. We thus still appear faced with the unenviable choice between the risk of world tyranny or continued international anarchy.

To assess whether there is any escape from this impasse, it may be helpful to explore further the alleged analogy between the state and an international state. Within a state a government also exercises a monopoly on the use of force to provide for the internal and external security of the realm. There is, therefore, a similar risk that a government may behave in a tyrannical manner towards its people. Within a state this problem is, in part, solved by the institution of elaborate checks and balances on the exercise of power resting, ultimately, in a democracy upon the ability of the majority to get rid, through the ballot box, of any individual who attempts to seize excessive power or to wield it to the detriment of the majority. It is thus perhaps possible to conceive of a similar system of checks and balances constraining the supranational authority's exercise of power, although it is difficult to envisage how the ultimate democratic constraint would be meaningfully exercised on a global scale.

But such controls are clearly only part of the solution. Philosophers have sometimes pictured states as coming into being solely to provide for the mutual protection of their members both from each other and external foes.[5] But such a fiction seems neither historically well founded nor intrinsically very plausible. If all that binds together the assumed egotistical and mistrustful members of such a community is their shared fear of anarchy without and law enforcement within, such a society would appear neither very

durable nor attractive. For the amount of coercive power required
to sustain order would be considerable, as would hence be the risk
either of its misuse or, in so far as that could be constrained by
checks and balances, of its ineffectiveness, given the assumed lack
of any underlying consensus of values to help define the occasions
on which the power should be exercised. It is, therefore, rather
more plausible to suppose that states come into being and persist
not simply because of a negative fear of anarchy but because of a
positive desire for community: a shared interest in living together
reflected, *inter alia*, in economic, cultural, religious and social ties
and underlain by common moral values. As Michael Walzer has
put it: 'Not army camps alone, as David Hume wrote, but temples,
storehouses, irrigation works and burial grounds are the true
mothers of cities.'[6] And it is because of this underlying consensus
that order can be maintained effectively without an excessive
coercive normative mechanism. For most people obey the law
because they are law-abiding, not simply through fear of
punishment.

These reflections suggest that a supranational authority charged
to preside over the external relations between states would need
enforcement powers but their exercise would need to be constrained
by checks and balances. Even more importantly, the authority
would need to grow out of and reflect an underlying community of
interest and consensus of values. Merely more extensive structural
change than Baruch envisaged — the superimposition of a fully-
fledged international security agency upon the world as it is —
would not of itself remove the distrust between nations upon which
the Baruch Plan foundered. Indeed, such structural change would
only appear either desirable or feasible if the distrust had already
been substantially reduced. And that, in turn, would require an
easing of the ideological, political and hegemonic rivalries between
states and a more equitable distribution of their share of the
planet's resources. With the grounds of inter-state conflict thus
reduced, so would the prospects for disarmament be increased,
together with the readiness of nation-states to surrender some of
their sovereignty to a supranational authority charged to supervise
the peaceful relations between states. Moreover, it is possible to
envisage that the process might acquire its own momentum. As the
distrust between states lessened, so would their readiness to
contemplate alternative methods of conflict resolution increase;
and, as international machinery to achieve this were established

and seen to work and the habit of co-operation in such shared political institutions became more rooted, so would the distrust lessen further and the community of interest grow. And more extensive structural change would then appear feasible.

Such a massive improvement in the relationships between states seems a distant and tenuous prospect. But so, no doubt, did the achievement of nationhood to the denizens of cities and so, from more recent history, must have appeared, at the close of the Second World War, even the current measure of unity between the states of Western Europe. Forty years ago it would have appeared hopelessly utopian to suppose that war between the major states of Western Europe would be — as it now is — virtually inconceivable. This unity has in part been maintained through the perception of a common foe to the east. But it also reflects the close ties of economic, cultural and political interest that have been developed and now help bind the states together. It is therefore perhaps not inconceivable that our global interdependence, to which lip-service is now paid, might one day become a reality, as nations perceive and act upon their bonds of common humanity and shared stewardship of the earth's resources and its future fate. It is, moreover, a goal eminently worth striving towards.

But have we even yet reached a stage at which nuclear weapons have been completely abolished? We are supposing a world in which the grounds of inter-state conflict have been reduced and from the growing consensus of interest has emerged an effective and benign supranational mechanism for maintaining peace. This transformation has enabled nations to feel sufficiently secure to reduce their conventional forces to a level required solely for internal security purposes and to abolish nuclear weapons from national armouries. Regular and reliable inspections are carried out to ensure the ban remains in force. But even in this radically transformed world, the risk would remain, however much reduced, that a nation might clandestinely re-acquire nuclear force and might then use or threaten to use its nuclear monopoly for wicked purposes and with devastating effect upon its disarmed neighbours. Nor would the supposition that a more just world order had been established remove this possibility: for it is a feature of the fallen condition of man that his greed could still motivate him to seek more than his fair share. To guard against this possibility it would therefore appear that the supranational authority would need to maintain at least some nuclear weapons. We have thus still failed to reach our goal of a nuclear-free world: we have merely changed the form but not the substance of deterrence. How then could that final step be achieved? Only, it would appear, by the very transformation of man's moral nature from which we earlier shied because its realisation appeared so remote.

A world completely free of nuclear weapons thus remains a distant and utopian vision. But it is a vision that neither our humanity nor Christian hope can allow us entirely to lose from sight. And perhaps the nearer we move towards it, the less intractable may seem the difficulties. But until the goal is within our grasp of a world from which nuclear weapons can be safely abolished at least from national armouries, we have no choice but to continue to rely on mutual deterrence between East and West to maintain peace.

This recognition is not an excuse for inaction. For there is much — of value in itself and as a move towards such a better international order — that can and should be done: to reduce the grounds of conflict, to lend more substance to the insight of our global interdependence and to improve the relations between states, above all, the Eastern and Western blocs that bestride the world. And a first step towards this would be the resumption of constructive political dialogue and serious arms control negotiations between the superpowers. But if complete nuclear disarmament is the ultimate goal, it is not the immediate objective of such negotiations: this is massively to reduce the nuclear stockpiles and to enhance the safety, stability and morality of deterrence.

NOTES

1. Deterrence

1. Bernard Brodie, 'The Atomic Bomb and American Security', Memorandum no. 18, Yale Institute of International Studies 1945, reprinted in Brodie (ed.), *The Absolute Weapon* (New York, Harcourt, Brace, 1946), p. 76.

2. *Statement on the Defence Estimates 1983*, Cmnd 8951, vol. 1 (London, HMSO, 1983), p. 4.

3. Desmond Ball, *Targeting for Strategic Deterrence*, Adelphi Papers no. 185 (London, International Institute for Strategic Studies, 1983).

4. *Report on FY 1975 Defense Budget and FY 1975–9 Defense Program.*

5. In a letter of 15 January 1983 to Cardinal Bernardin, quoted in 'The Challenge of Peace: God's Promise and Our Response', A Pastoral Letter on War and Peace, the National Conference of US Catholic Bishops, 3 May 1983, reprinted in Philip J. Murnion (ed.), *Catholics and Nuclear War* (London, Geoffrey Chapman, 1983), p. 300 note 81.

6. *The Future United Kingdom Strategic Nuclear Deterrent Force*, HMG Defence Open Government Document 80/23, p. 6.

7. There is no convenient precise definition of the terms 'strategic' and 'theatre' nuclear weapons. The usual practical working definition is that strategic nuclear weapons are those defined as such in draft Article II of the SALT II Treaty; the rest are theatre weapons. On this basis, strategic forces comprise broadly very long-range intercontinental systems, including land-based missiles, submarine-launched missiles and long-range bombers; theatre systems those of less than intercontinental range primarily based in Europe.

8. Michael Howard, 'The Relevance of Traditional Strategy', *Foreign Affairs*, vol. 51, no. 2, January 1973, p. 262.

9. The concept of 'strategic defence' was explored by President Reagan in an address on 23 March 1983.

10. Thomas C. Schelling, *The Strategy of Conflict* (Cambridge, Mass., Harvard University Press, 1963), p. 260.

11. Bernard Brodie, *War and Politics* (New York, Macmillan, 1973), p. 431.

2. The Just War Tradition I

1. Christine de Pisan, *Fayttes of Armes*, I.2.

2. The history of the tradition is well covered by F. H. Russell, *The Just War in the Middle Ages* (Cambridge University Press, 1975); James Turner Johnson, *Ideology, Reason and the Limitation of War* (Princeton University Press, 1975), *Just War Tradition and the Restraint of War* (Princeton University Press, 1981).

3. See for example, John C. Ford S.J., 'Morality of Obliteration Bombing', *Theological Studies*, vol. 5, 1944 reprinted in Richard A. Wasserstrom (ed.), *War and Morality* (Belmont, California, Wadsworth Publishing, 1970); Paul Ramsey, *War and Christian Conscience* (Durham, N.C., Duke University Press, 1961), *The Just War: Force and Political Responsibility* (New York, Charles Scribner's Sons, 1968). A recent comprehensive exposition of the theory is contained in William V.

O'Brien, *The Conduct of Just and Limited War* (New York, Praeger, 1981).
4. 'The Challenge of Peace: God's Promise and Our Response', reprinted in Philip J. Murnion (ed.), *Catholics and Nuclear War*.
5. *The Church and the Bomb*: the report of a working party under the chairmanship of the Bishop of Salisbury (London, Hodder and Stoughton, 1982).
6. Michael Walzer, *Just and Unjust Wars* (London, Allen Lane, 1977), esp. ch. 2.
7. St Augustine, *City of God*, XIX, 7 in Whitney J. Oates (ed.), *Basic Writings of St Augustine* (New York, Random House, 1948).
8. St Aquinas, *Summa Theologica*, II/II q.40 art.1 in A. P. D'Entreves (ed.), *Aquinas: Selected Political Writings* (Oxford, Basil Blackwell, 1948).
9. Jonathan Barnes, 'The Just War' in N. Kretzmann, A. Kenny, J. Pinborg (eds.), *The Cambridge History of Later Medieval Philosophy* (Cambridge University Press, 1982).
10. Francisco de Vitoria, *de Jure Belli*, 13.
11. James Turner Johnson, *Ideology, Reason and the Limitation of War*.
12. Vitoria, *de Jure Belli*, 21 who counsels the wise prince 'to consult the good and wise and those who speak with freedom and without anger or bitterness or greed'.
13. Barrie Paskins and Michael Dockrill, *The Ethics of War* (London, Duckworth, 1977), p. 216.
14. 'The Challenge of Peace: God's Promise and Our Response' in *Catholics and Nuclear War*, p. 278.
15. Walzer, *Just and Unjust Wars*, p. 121.
16. Vitoria, *de Jure Belli*, 37.
17. Walzer, *Just and Unjust Wars*, p. 129.
18. B. H. Liddell Hart, *Strategy: the Indirect Approach* (London, Faber and Faber, 1968), p. 334 (emphasis added).
19. Aquinas, *Summa Theologica*, quoting Romans 13:4 (The translation used is that of the New English Bible).
20. Paul Ramsey 'The Case for Making "Just War" possible' in John C. Bennett (ed.), *Nuclear Weapons and the Conflict of Conscience* (London, Butterworth Press, 1962), p. 148.
21. *Catholics and Nuclear War*, p. 282.

3. The Just War Tradition II

1. For the history of the principle of non-combatant immunity see James Turner Johnson, *Ideology, Reason and the Limitation of War* and *Just War Tradition and the Restraint of War*. The thirteenth-century treatise *De Treuga et Pace* (of Truces and Peace) proposed immunity to: clerics, monks, friars, other religious, pilgrims, travellers, merchants and peasants cultivating the soil.
2. A concise history of the principle of double effect is found in the Appendix 'The History of Intention in Ethics' to Anthony Kenny, *The Anatomy of the Soul* (Oxford, Basil Blackwell, 1973).
3. Elizabeth Anscombe, 'War and Murder' reprinted in R. A. Wasserstrom (ed.), *War and Morality*, p. 50.
4. Discussed by Anthony Kenny, *Will, Freedom and Power* (Oxford, Basil Blackwell, 1975), p. 62.
5. H. L. A. Hart, *Punishment and Responsibility* (Oxford at the University Press, 1968), pp. 119–20.
6. P. F. Strawson, 'Freedom and Resentment' reprinted in Strawson (ed.),

Studies in the Philosophy of Thought and Action (London, Oxford University Press, 1968), p. 75.

7. For discussion of these cases see, for example, Hart, *Punishment and Responsibility*; Philippa Foot, 'Problems of Abortion and the Doctrine of Double Effect' reprinted in Foot, *Virtues and Vices and Other Essays in Moral Philosophy* (Oxford, Basil Blackwell, 1978); Jonathan Bennett, 'Whatever the Consequences', *Analysis*, vol. 26, 1965–6; Jonathan Glover, *Causing Deaths and Saving Lives* (London, Allen Lane, 1977), ch. 6.

8. This is a slight variation from the usual supposition that, in the craniotomy case, the foetus could be delivered alive by a post-mortem operation if the craniotomy is not performed and the mother is allowed to die.

9. Quoted Hart, *Punishment and Responsibility*, p. 120.

10. See, for example, Anthony Kenny, 'Intention and Mens Rea in Murder' in P. M. S. Hacker and J. Raz (eds.), *Law, Morality and Society — Essays in Honour of H. L. A. Hart* (Oxford at the University Press, 1977).

11. Quoted by Walzer, *Just and Unjust Wars*, p. 152.

12. Catholic theologians had sought to argue that the foetus could be regarded as a 'combatant': a view quashed by the ruling of the Holy Office of 28 May 1884 that in no case may a uterine foetus be regarded as a materially unjust aggressor. Discussed by Paul Ramsey, *War and the Christian Conscience*, ch. 8.

13. J. J. C. Smart and Bernard Williams, *Utilitarianism For and Against* (Cambridge at the University Press, 1973), pp. 98–9.

14. Barrie Paskins and Michael Dockrill, *The Ethics of War*, p. 233.

15. Discussed by Foot, *Virtues and Vices*.

16. Williams Ames, 'Conscience, with the Power and Cases Thereof', Quest. 6, 33 A.4 quoted by Johnson, *Ideology, Reason and the Limitation of War*, p. 199.

17. Quoted Walzer, *Just and Unjust Wars*, p. 259.

18. Ibid., p. 261.

19. The official historians of the RAF offensive note that: 'the moral issue was not really an operative factor. The choice between precision and area bombing was not conditioned by abstract theories of right and wrong, nor by interpretations of international law. It was ruled by operational possibilities and strategic intentions.' Sir Charles Webster and Noble Frankland, *The Strategic Air Offensive Against Germany, 1939–45* (London, HMSO, 1961), vol. II, p. 22.

4. Just War and Nuclear Weapons

1. Congress of the United States Office of Technology Assessment, *The Effects of Nuclear War* (Washington, US Government Printing Office, 1979).

2. Ibid., p. 86.

3. Described by Carl Sagan, 'Nuclear War and Climatic Catastrophe: Some Policy Implications', *Foreign Affairs*, vol. 62, no. 2, Winter 1983/4, pp. 257–92.

5. Alternatives to Deterrence

1. Such measures are advocated, for example, by Bruce Kent, 'A Christian Unilateralism', in G. Goodwin (ed.), *Ethics and Nuclear Deterrence* (London, Croom Helm, 1982); the establishment of a nuclear weapons free zone 'from Poland to Portugal' is the aim of the European Nuclear Disarmament Campaign, as expounded by E. P. Thompson and others in E. P. Thompson and Dan Smith

(eds.), *Protest and Survive* (Harmondsworth, Middlesex, Penguin, 1980).
2. President Reagan, 23 March 1983.
3. These differences are explored in detail by Gregory S. Kavka, 'Deterrence, Utility and Rational Choice', *Theory and Decision* vol. 12, 1980.

6. Deterrence and Intentions

1. G. E. M. Anscombe, *Intention* (Oxford, Basil Blackwell, 1957), §1.
2. Donald Davidson, *Actions and Events* (Oxford, Clarendon Press, 1980), p. 83.
3. Ibid., p. 100.
4. S. Hampshire, *Thought and Action* (London, Chatto and Windus, 1959), p. 134.
5. J. Feinberg, 'Action and Responsibility' in M. Black (ed.), *Philosophy in America* (Ithaca, Cornell University Press, 1965).
6. Anscombe, *Intention*, §23.
7. Discussed by Eric D'Arcy, *Human Acts* (Oxford, Clarendon Press, 1963), ch. 4, part 3.
8. Thus characterised by Sir Arthur Hockaday, 'In Defence of Deterrence' in G. Goodwin (ed.), *Ethics and Nuclear Deterrence* (London, Croom Helm, 1982).
9. Barrie Paskins, 'Deep Cuts are Morally Imperative' in Ibid., p. 99.
10. Davidson, *Actions and Events*, p. 84.
11. Barrie Paskins and Michael Dockrill, *The Ethics of War* (London, Duckworth, 1979), p. 71.
12. *New York Review of Books*, 16 June 1983.
13. The claim is made, for example, by Father Francis X. Winters, S.J. in a letter to *Commentary*, vol. 76, no. 6, December 1983.
14. Paskins, 'Deep Cuts are Morally Imperative', pp. 98–9.
15. 'The Challenge of Peace: God's Promise and Our Response', A Pastoral Letter on War and Peace, 3 May 1983, National Conference of US Catholic Bishops, reprinted in Philip J. Murnion (ed.), *Catholics and Nuclear War* (London, Geoffrey Chapman, 1983), pp. 245–344. There is dispute among exegetes of the bishops' somewhat ambiguous text whether *any* use is ruled out, although it does appear that any militarily meaningful use is so excluded. On this, see, for example, the exchange of letters between Father Winters, Bruce Russett and Albert Wohlstetter in *Commentary*, vol. 76, no. 6, December 1983.
16. Thus argued by Gregory S. Kavka, 'Some Paradoxes of Deterrence', *Journal of Philosophy*, vol. LXXV, no. 6, June 1978.
17. Discussed by Richard Harries, 'Morality of Nuclear Deterrence' in R. Harries (ed.), *What Hope in an Armed World?* (Basingstoke, Pickering and Inglis, 1982, pp. 100–1).

7. Deterrence and Use

1. J. Newhouse, *Cold Dawn: The Story of SALT* (New York, Holt, Rinehart and Winston, 1973), p. 176.
2. Fred Charles Iklé, 'Can Deterrence Last Out the Century?', *Foreign Affairs*, vol. 51, no. 2, January 1973, p. 279. See also David Alan Rosenberg, 'The Origins of Overkill: Nuclear Weapons and American Strategy 1945–1960', *International Security*, vol. 7, no. 4, Spring 1983.

3. Bernard Brodie, *Strategy in the Missile Age* (London, Oxford University Press, 1959), p. 276.

4. McGeorge Bundy, 'To Cap the Volcano', *Foreign Affairs*, vol. 48, no. 1, October 1969, pp. 9–10.

5. Laurence Martin, *The Two Edged Sword*, Reith Lectures 1981 (London, Weidenfeld and Nicholson, 1982), p. 20.

6. Bernard Brodie, *Escalation and the Nuclear Option* (Princeton University Press, 1966), p. 37. The difficulties for escalation control are well argued in: Desmond Ball, *Can Nuclear War Be Controlled?*, Adelphi Papers no. 169 (London, International Institute for Strategic Studies, 1981); Paul Bracken, *The Command and Control of Nuclear Forces* (New Haven, Yale University Press, 1983).

7. As Col. M. Shirokov observed in 1966, 'the objective is not to turn the large economic and industrial regions into a heap of ruins': cited in Joseph Douglas, Jr., *Soviet Military Strategy in Europe* (New York, Pergamon Press, 1980), p. 26.

8. Thomas C. Schelling, *The Strategy of Conflict* (Cambridge, Mass., Harvard University Press, 1963), p. 260.

9. A recent survey of some of these developments is in Stephen M. Meyer, 'Soviet Theatre Nuclear Forces Part I: Development of Doctrine and Objectives', Adelphi Papers no. 187, Winter 1983/4.

10. Raymond L. Garthoff, *Soviet Strategy in the Nuclear Age* (New York, Praeger, 1958), p. 11.

11. Maj.-Gen. V. I. Zemskov, cited in Douglas, *Soviet Military Strategy*, p. 162.

8. Some Policy Implications

1. For example, McGeorge Bundy, George F. Kennan, Robert McNamara, Gerald Smith, 'Nuclear Weapons and the Atlantic Alliance', *Foreign Affairs*, vol. 60, no. 3, Spring 1982.

2. Robert S. McNamara, 'The Military Role of Nuclear Weapons', *Foreign Affairs*, vol. 62, no. 1, Fall 1983.

3. Ibid., p. 78.

4. *Whence the Threat to Peace?* (Moscow, 1982), p. 74.

5. A point well made by Bernard Brodie, *Escalation and the Nuclear Option*, p. 84.

6. Quoted in M. Walzer, *Just and Unjust Wars*, p. 256.

7. George Urban, 'A Conversation with George F. Kennan', 47 *Encounter* 3: 37, September 1976.

8. These developments are enthusiastically described in the *Report of the European Security Study: Strengthening Conventional Deterrence in Europe — Proposals for the 1980s* (London, Macmillan Press, 1983). A more balanced approach is taken in the essay 'New Technology, New Tactics', *Statement on the Defence Estimates 1983*, Cmnd 8951, vol. 1 (London, HMSO, 1983), p. 24.

9. Conclusions and a Vision for the Future

1. Quoted Bernard G. Bechhoefer, *Postwar Negotiations for Arms Control* (Washington, D.C., The Brookings Institution, 1961), p. 30.

2. K. N. Waltz, *Theory of International Politics* (Reading, Mass., Addison-Wesley, 1979).

3. I. Kant, *Perpetual Peace — A Philosophical Sketch* in Hans Reiss (ed.), *Kant's Political Writings* (Cambridge University Press, 1970), pp. 93–130. The reference to 'soulless despotism' is on p. 113.

4. Ibid., p. 104.

5. A recent example is Robert Nozick, *Anarchy, State and Utopia* (Oxford, Basil Blackwell, 1974).

6. M. Walzer, *Spheres of Justice* (Oxford, Martin Robertson, 1983), p. 65.

INDEX